About the Author

Catherine Ryan Howard is an occasionally delusional twenty-something from Cork, Ireland. As well as working in Walt Disney World, Catherine has administrated things in the Netherlands, cleaned tents on a French campsite, established a handmade card company and answered telephones in *several* different offices.

She is currently working on a novel, daydreaming of a US Green Card and drinking way too much coffee.

She wants to be a NASA astronaut when she grows up.

Visit her blog at **www.catherineryanhoward.com**.

CATHERINE RYAN HOWARD

MOUSETRAPPED

A Year and A Bit in Orlando, Florida

MOUSETRAPPED
A Year and A Bit in Orlando, Florida

MOUSETRAPPED

Prologue
LABOR DAY

On the night of September 4th, 2006, I was at home in Cork, Ireland, utterly unable to sleep.

Across the room, my enormous purple suitcase was packed to the zips with summer clothes, anti-frizz hair products and bottles of sunscreen. Leaning against it, my carry-on bag. This held my computer, my journal, two books, twice as many magazines as I could feasibly read during an eight-hour flight, and a fetching pair of fluffy pink slipper socks. Stuffed into an envelope were my passport, my US visa documents and proof of my imminent employment in a Walt Disney World hotel. Photocopies were hidden in various other places; I was taking no chances with the Department of Homeland Security.

The alarm clock was set for five, allowing plenty of time for me to get up, get caffeinated, get my hair straightened and get to the airport, only a five minute drive from my home. My first flight would take me to London Gatwick, the second all the way to Orlando, Florida.

I'd got the job offer in May; it had been a long, impatient wait riddled with excitement. I had never even been to Florida before and I couldn't wait to see the sunshine, palm trees and long, sandy beaches that my *Rough Guide* promised would be there in abundance.

But it wasn't only anticipation that was keeping me awake.

Just before I went to bed, I made the mistake of reading my horoscope for the coming week online. It predicted that on Wednesday - my first full day in Orlando - I would learn something that would 'change everything' and that for the next month I'd be spending a lot of time at home on my own.

Say *what* now?

The following evening I would land in Orlando with one suitcase and no place to live, knowing just one other soul on the entire continent - my cousin David would be 900 miles to the north in Towson, Maryland. Yet I was convinced that it would be mere days before a smiling, suntanned and inexplicably skinnier me would be skipping around Magic Kingdom, wearing a Tinkerbell T-shirt and towing behind me a gaggle of new, fun friends. Someone would think to snap a candid photo of our happy faces which, later, I'd place in a Mickey Mouse-shaped frame and hang somewhere prominent, a reminder of the darned fantastic time I'd had in the happiest place on earth.

I thought that building a whole new life for yourself in a foreign land thousands of miles from home would be just like preparing a Pot Noodle: easy and instant.

Of course, it didn't work out that way.

Unbeknownst to me, I was about to be whacked across the face with a cold, wet fish called Reality. For the first time in my life I'd struggle on a daily basis. It would be months before I'd set as much as a toe in Magic Kingdom and, worst of all, that stupid horoscope would be proven to have been exactly right.

Lucky for you, as this would have been a ceaselessly boring book otherwise.

PART I
An Irish Girl in a Disney World

One
THE CALL OF THE MOUSE

Once upon a time, in a land that could be far, far away from you depending on your current geographical location, there lived a little girl who believed that the best way to stand out from the crowd was to dream big - to dream *specific* - and not to let a little thing called reality get in the way.

Our story begins in the week before Christmas, nineteen hundred and ninety-five.

I was dutifully following my parents around on a last minute shopping trip when somewhere among the pungent deodorant gift sets and the festive biscuit tins comprised mainly of varieties that people didn't care to eat, I spotted an interesting paperback.

It had a quote on the cover from Mr. Stephen King who claimed that the book was 'the most horrifying true story' he had ever read. The previous summer I had laboured my way through King's *The Stand* and had been sufficiently terrorised by it to now conclude that this book must indeed be truly horrifying. So I picked up a copy and initiated Operation Nag Dad. He (eventually) agreed to buy it for me and the rest is history.

Or at least, the rest is the rest of this book.

It was *The Hot Zone* by Richard Preston, a somewhat sensationalised account of an outbreak of the Ebola virus in Reston, Virginia, in 1989. According to Preston, a highly virulent and deadly disease that just loved to liquefy internal organs and turn eyeballs into a bloody mush had reared its head 'in the shadow of the White House.'

It was actually a strain that only infected monkeys, Reston is over twenty miles from the White House and the entire incident was confined to small animal storage facility, but *still*.

Before I'd even reached the book's end, I knew I had just stumbled upon my vocation. There was no doubt about it; I simply *had* to become a virologist.

But not just any virologist, oh no. I had to be the kind that worked with viral haemorrhagic fevers in the Biosafety Level 4 laboratories of the United States Army Medical Research Institute of Infectious Diseases (USAMRIID) in Fort Detrick, Maryland.

I would find ways to overcome the more obvious hurdles – not being an American citizen, not being in the US Army, being too squeamish to handle raw chicken – and then my dream life would be mine, just like that.

I shared my plans with anyone who would listen, and some who didn't care to.

I was thirteen years old at the time.

By now you're probably wondering what in the name of Donald Duck this has to do with me working in Walt Disney World, and I can hardly blame you. Virulent haemorrhagic fevers and Mickey Mouse are hardly bedfellows, unless you consider the rodent angle. But I can assure you that my Disney decision does indeed have its roots in disease.

Telling Grown-Ups that you're going to be a virologist is not like telling them that you're planning to get a job in a bank or the civil service. After you explain what it is – the initial reaction is invariably a blank stare and a, 'What's that?' – they start to look at you differently. Eyebrows go north; faces become thoughtful; there is many an intrigued listening noise made. Aunts and uncles look vaguely horrified as you tell them about how you want to be encased in a biohazard suit and locked in an airless chamber with a cousin of the bubonic plague on a daily basis for all the working years of your adult life. They shoot a look at your mother who just rolls her eyes and shakes her head because this is, let's not forget, the same daughter who demanded to be taken to see *Philadelphia* when she was only eleven and so this is exactly the kind of precocious, crazed behaviour you've come to expect.

I felt special, singled out from the crowd. While everyone else was blabbing on about careers that all basically boiled down to paperwork and coffee breaks, I was saving the world – although, alas, not innocent monkeys - from microbes which had starring roles in *Outbreak*. When I told people what I wanted to do with my life I got a reaction. If I ever were to actually become a virologist, I could solicit that same reaction from every person who ever asked what it was I did for a living. It was like telling people that you were a NASA astronaut or an FBI agent. I would be *interesting*; a hit at dinner parties; the clear winner in any game of What Does Your Daughter/Sister/Wife Do.

And so I began to prepare.

I assembled a small collection of virologist memoirs (yes, there are such things), bought *Outbreak* on video (squealing every time at the shot of USAMRIID) and used our brand new home internet service to download such wondrous things as the *Weekly Morbidity and Mortality Report* published by Atlanta's Centres for Disease Control (CDC). I managed to turn every English essay assignment into a story involving disease. My entry into the 1998 Young Science Writers' Competition traced the origins of AIDS along Central African highways. When Dr Robert Gallo, co-discoverer of HIV, came to University College Cork, I sat in the front row of the lecture hall, resisting the urge to scream like a tween at a Jonas Brothers concert and failing to hear a single word he said; I was so awed by the presence of a real, live virologist that the sound of my own frenetic heartbeat drowned out that of his voice.

When I was in my fourth year of secondary school and aged sixteen, each of us had to visit our career guidance counsellor and declare what it was we planned to do with the rest of our lives. After I told her about my future as a world-renowned virologist, the counsellor took off her glasses, sat back in her chair and said that in the course of her long and illustrious career at Regina Mundi College, no one else had *ever* told her anything like that.

And there it was: confirmation. I now had evidence, as I saw it, that I was somehow better than the hundreds of other girls who had sat in that same plastic chair, tugged nervously at their ugly purple uniform and confided that they intended to join the trouser-suited masses; to be paid to complete routine administrative tasks such as answering the telephone and stapling things together; to use their unimpressive salaries to buy boxy semi-detached houses near their parents; to marry some guy with a trade who would have developed a beer belly before they even got back from the honeymoon, with whom they'd dutifully produce two or three miniature versions of themselves with whom they'd take a cheap sun holiday every August for the next eighteen years or so; to arrive in twenty years' time to our class reunion in a reliable family car with crumbs in the back seat, a low-maintenance haircut they got at a chain salon on student night and a colour they'd put in themselves, and they wouldn't touch the cheesecake because it had too many Points in it and they'd a Communion coming up, and - most pathetic of all to my teenage mind - they would be satisfied with all this, maybe even *happy*.

I hadn't so much decided to become a virologist as I had rejected the idea of doing anything less spectacular. There was no way now I could consider a future in which Adult Me was a bank teller, a nurse or an office worker trapped in a generic cube farm.

When people dared to question how I could possibly go from being an average student ('could do better' was the theme of my entire academic career) in a small suburban school in Cork to being a world famous virologist with a PhD from Johns Hopkins and dual Irish-American citizenship, I turned my ears off. I knew it was going to happen; the logistics were unimportant. I was in pursuit of my wild and exotic dreams – and with them, wild and exotic diseases – and had no time for any protests on reality's behalf.

We were to be the class of 2001, the first graduates of the New Millennium. We were perched on the very cusp of greatness, destined for bright and wonderful futures filled with limitless possibility, awesome adventure and ultimately, complete fulfilment.

Why, in the face of all that, would we turn around and become a *travel agent*?

Of course these days, I'm not quite a virologist.

That's why the name of this book isn't *Fever Pitch, My Germ-Filled Life*, or *Gee, I Really Hope I Don't Accidentally Stick Myself With a Needle Full of Ebola Virus Today*; or any of the other fabulous titles I had prepared for my own virologist memoir. It's not because I stopped wanting to be one, though. It's because when the time came to actually do something about my dream besides practising signing my name with a 'Dr' in front of it, I took the easy road and decided to give up the dream instead.

As we daydreamed our way through the end of our schooldays my friends and I imagined that soon, everything we wanted would be ours. We spent lunchtimes discussing our plans for world domination. Step one: Go to college. Step two: Land dream job as Irish civilian virologist at US Army facility. Step three: Wake up one morning skinny, rich and alongside gorgeous quantum physicist husband who reads, has excellent DNA and shows no real interest in televised sports. Once I'd all that sorted out, I'd then accidentally stumble upon a brand new virus, a vaccine *and* a cure for it, all in the same day. (Maybe even all before lunch.) There'd be a library named after me in no time.

But back in reality, things didn't work out that way.

The beginning of the end was my impressive failing of the Leaving Cert Biology exam. Never one to do things by halves, there was no mediocre C or low D; I just about got an E, the Microbiology section a suspicious outburst of knowledge in an otherwise unused answer book. Since I'd spent the first five years of my secondary education daydreaming about joining the CDC's Epidemiology Intelligence Service and becoming the virologist equivalent of Special Agent Scully, and then the last year of it daydreaming about a boy, the rest of my results were hardly anything to write home about either.

People, justifiably, were confused. Hadn't I just spent my entire adolescence talking about becoming a virologist? Isn't that the kind of thing that someone who got straight As, or a maximum score of 600 points, or the best grades in all of Ireland would do, and not some dreamy slacker who failed Biology, never did her French homework and only got a B in Ordinary Level Math?

I still managed to get into college, albeit by the skin of my teeth. I had applied to a university in the north west of England for a place on their Combined Science degree course, where I had planned to double major in Biology and Psychology. They had extended a conditional offer: a place in exchange for 430 Leaving Cert points and a pass in five Higher Level subjects. Not only had Biology been one of those Higher five, but my total points score amounted to a paltry 395.

The morning of the results, my mother called the university's Admissions Department.

'Ah, yes,' the nice Admissions lady said after a minute. 'Catherine has been offered a place on our Combined Science degree program.'

This left my mother a tad confused, as she had just had me on the phone wailing about being thirty-five points short of a university education.

'But she was told she needed 430,' my mother pressed. 'She only got 395.'

There was a long, pregnant pause before the woman said, 'Mrs Howard, Catherine has been offered a place on our Combined Science program. I don't know what to tell you, but I'd recommend you don't ask any questions.'

She didn't, and neither did I. When the offer came through online I printed out a couple of copies, just in case. Then, on the last day of September 2001, I flew across the Irish Sea and took up my place in university.

Three weeks later, I dropped out. Although as one of those three weeks was the alcohol-fuelled, lecture-free Freshers' Week, I technically only stayed for two.

At the time I claimed there were many complex reasons behind my dramatic exit from third level education, but really there was only ever one. I had found out that it was hard to get the things we want and that the universe wasn't necessarily going to do us any favours while we pursued them. In the harsh light of this new information, I decided I just couldn't be bothered even trying and abruptly gave up.

If I invited in reality, I was forced to acknowledge that it was extremely unlikely I would ever get to do the kind of virology work I dreamed of doing. Even with a lifetime of hard graft, sacrifice and perseverance it might never happen, and I wanted a guarantee before I went and put in all the effort. In other words, I wanted a Commander's seat on the Space Shuttle before I even filled out the Astronaut Corps application.

And I *did* let reality in.

I thought being realistic was what being an adult was all about.

So I trudged back to Cork, moved in with my then boyfriend – who didn't even read newspapers – and took up a minimum wage job as a sales assistant in a greeting card store as well as my new role as the black sheep of the Howard family.

The girl who had once considered herself destined for biohazard suits and the World Health Organisation was now dressed in an ill-fitting department store's own brand blazer and attending staff meetings of great importance, such as the one in which we discussed what size paper bag to use for a standard-sized card, because if you made a slit down the side of the smallest bag, you could fit a standard card in there and then tape it back up, avoiding the use of a medium-sized bag and saving the store untold amounts of money, perhaps as much as tens of euro annually.

(Seriously. There was an actual meeting about that and, worse still, that was the meeting's *only topic*.)

Every morning I wanted to gouge out my eyeballs with a blunt pencil just so I'd have a valid excuse to stay home from work. We couldn't afford the apartment we were renting and began to dig ourselves a hole of credit card debt. Socialising was far too expensive so we grew distant from our friends and soon the highlight of our week was a Mexican dinner and an episode of *The West Wing*. I started to pile on the pounds and actually did, one New Year, resort to joining Weight Watchers.

One day I woke up to find I'd become my own worst nightmare. Through inaction, I had chosen a path along which there seemed to be no opportunity to make a U-turn. I doubted there was anywhere else I could go anyway. I tried to make peace with this new reality, the one in which my one-time dizzyingly bright future was now decidedly more grey and commonplace. I began to believe that this was the only outcome that had ever been on the cards and to think any differently had indeed been dreaming.

Stay with me. We'll have our Mouse Ears on soon, I promise.

I turned twenty-two in the summer of 2004 and was by that point so bored with my own life that I would have changed the channel if that's what had been showing on TV. I was working as a secretary in an auctioneers' office, The Boyfriend and I had just passed the four year point in our relationship, and I was finding it harder and harder to get out of bed in the mornings - it just didn't seem worth the effort.

With all my dreams stowed away in a drawer, I was unsettled by the utter predictability of it all. Unless I did something drastic, I more or less knew where I'd be one, two, ten years from now and so did everyone else. I'd be right here in Cork, doing the same thing I was doing today. I might have a wedding band, a child, or an obsessive scrap-booking hobby, but the big picture would remain the same.

I knew I could never *ever* make my peace with that.

My best friend, Sheelagh, whose adventurous single life I envied even more than her tiny waist, had recently upped and moved to the Greek island of Crete. One night I took a deep breath and before I could think too much about the consequences, I asked The Boyfriend how he would feel if I went and joined her there for, say, three months.

Can open, worms everywhere, to steal a line from *Friends*.

Having met as teenagers, our fledgling adult selves now wanted different things than we had when we were seventeen - hell, we wanted things we didn't even know about when we were seventeen - and whatever they might be, it certainly wasn't each other. And so, after the most amicable break-up in the history of mankind, I was young, free and single and thanks to my credit card bills, totally broke.

For a few days I was fine; my world was all possibility and Beyoncé songs. But two weeks in I found myself gripped by a sudden panic. I couldn't afford to quit my job and move to Greece, so nothing had really changed. I was still stuck in Cork, only now I was stuck there alone. I spent three straight days on the sofa with a stack of romantic comedies and a box of Kleenex, crying in cycles: silent tears, heaving sobs, ghoulish wails. Of course, it didn't help that The Ex-Boyfriend had taken to singledom like a duck to water (or like a twenty-three year old guy single for the first time in his adult life) while I sat at home with only calories for friends.

Needing to get away for a while, I coerced my family into letting me tag along on their Keycamp holiday to Paris.

Keycamp is a company that operates self-drive, family-orientated holidays on campsites throughout Europe. Not to be confused with *actual* camping, this usually involves driving yourself, your family and a fortnight's supply of Cornflakes onto a plush passenger ferry which deposits you hundreds of miles from your destination, leaving you to find your own way to the needle in a French haystack that is your chosen site (and this, ladies and gentlemen, was before the days of Sat Nav) where you'll spend the next two weeks in a fully-equipped mobile home pretending you are roughing it. Every couple of summers during my childhood we were taken on one of these holidays and although we may have failed miserably to fully appreciate them at the time, they were undeniably brilliant.

On this occasion however, not so much.

The sky was overcast every day, we only went into the city once and there were five of us – Mum, Dad, my brother John and my sister Claire – squeezed into a 'Classic' mobile home, one hundred and fifty square feet if you included the shower tray.

But, not to get all dramatic about it, this holiday would change the course of my entire life.

The campsite was staffed with friendly college-age kids who were inexplicably called 'couriers'. They cleaned the accommodation, welcomed you to the site and were generally available at all times of the day and night to provide you with directions, change your gas bottle or lay claim to that box of *steak haché* you were planning on leaving behind. They were paid a pittance, which was compensated for by the provision of on-site accommodation, a fetching uniform of T-shirt and shorts and the warm, self-satisfied feeling that comes from spending a summer living and working abroad.

One morning my mother returned from Reception, where she'd been annoying our couriers for directions to Versailles and admiring photos of the team enjoying a day out in Paris.

'I bet they have a great time,' she remarked casually.

The sentence echoed in my mind; I thought so too. In fact, the more I thought about it, the more I thought I should apply to be a courier the following summer. That would give me time to pay off my bills while having something up ahead to look forward to. I'd be living and working overseas, I'd meet loads of new people and with any luck, I'd return home with a tan. I sent in an application and thus my adventures began.

Oh, and the wailing on the sofa?

That was just PMS.

We're getting close!

At the interview with Keycamp's parent company, Holidaybreak, I was offered a better job than the one I'd applied for: administrator at the courier training facility in the Netherlands. Not only was this more money, but it was a job that a) I was qualified to do and b) didn't involve gas bottles. Moreover, it started sooner - in February - and Sheelagh, having moved from Crete to

Amsterdam, would only be an hour and a half away from me by train.

I went on to work not one but two seasons in Hoeven, a tiny village/glorified crossroads in the south of the country where each year around fifteen hundred new couriers are trained for their onsite roles. Having never worked abroad before, I got a serious case of The First Seasons: deliriously happy with my ten or so new best friends, our Dutch life and the exoticness of living in a foreign land, albeit one that had the BBC, Waterstones and English-speaking citizens. Even though elements of the job were nightmarish, we could always say, 'Well, at least we're not at home.'

And it had been so *easy*. I wanted the job; I applied for it; I got it; I packed up and moved to the Netherlands. It was like a whole new life presented as an IKEA flat pack, but better; there was no assembly required.

It occurred to me that maybe all those other things I had wanted to do could be as easily achieved as well.

I thought back to the childhood and teenage dreams I'd accumulated over the years, other than becoming a virologist. Chronologically they went something like this: to be a writer, to be a NASA astronaut, to be a professional dancer, to work for the FBI in their Behavioural Science Unit at Quantico, Virginia, to be a personal assistant to a Formula 1 driver, to work for Microsoft, to be a White House aide, to work for Disney in one of their theme parks.

I can also pinpoint the origin of each of these fanciful notions: learning to read; the movie *Space Camp*; *Top of the Pops*; Patricia Cornwell novels; realising that F1 World Champion Jacques Villeneuve was absolutely gorgeous; finding *Hard Drive: Bill Gates and the Making of the Microsoft Empire* marked down in a second-hand bookshop; a present of a *West Wing* box set, and an episode of *Changing Rooms* where the designers transformed the Parisian apartment of two Disneyland employees with interesting-sounding jobs.

There were also the more generalised ambitions of seeing the world, sporting a permatan and maybe, one day, living and working in the United States - a country I considered to be my spiritual home based solely on daydreams and ten days in New York.

But I didn't want Virology Round 2 - I had no interest in setting myself up for disappointment - and a few of those dreams required that I become an American citizen, or least find an American citizen to marry, as well as a few other talents I was guessing I didn't possess. (For one thing, I don't think nervous flyers make very good astronauts, and there's *a lot* further to fall.) Which left me with just one thing, and that was working for Disney.

I thought it would be a fun, interesting thing to do. I thought it sounded cool. I'd been to Disneyland Paris twice and all the staff I'd encountered there had just looked so goddamn happy. Alas, *mon francais était horrible*, since I'd spent six years of French classes drawing Ebola virus particles on the pages of my *Bienvenue en France* textbook.

Disney *World*, however, the Florida-based home of Disney's kingdom, would not only satisfy the Disney requirement but would have the added bonuses of sunny weather and the United States. And although it wouldn't be astronaut training or a summer at Space Camp, it'd put me a mere sixty miles from Kennedy Space Centre.

And then there were the Grown-Ups. I was one myself now too – allegedly - but I still looked to the older crowd for validation, for the nod that would confirm I was indeed on the right path. Thus far, I had failed to keep my word, dropped out of college after only three weeks, lived in sin with my boyfriend for nearly three years and not yet seen much more than the minimum wage on a pay-check. Those days when I'd been able to bask in approval and admiration were long gone, if they'd ever existed in the first place. Working in Holland had elevated me somewhat but there were still a lot of adults out there who I'd failed to impress.

I was convinced that *I'm going to go work in Disney World* would be the line to do it.

I searched the Disney World website for information. The resort ran two main recruitment programs that kept its parks and hotels staffed with an army of fun-loving youths prepared to work for pennies in exchange for an all-access Disney pass and the Florida sunshine: the College Program and the International Program. The College Program (CP) does exactly what it says on the tin, recruiting graduates from relative fields of study - business, hospitality, culinary, etc. - to work in various positions around the resorts; it was why the girl whose job it was to wave at you as you departed on your ride up Big Thunder Mountain had a degree in Operations Management under her Minnie belt. Meanwhile, the International Program (IP) added a layer of authenticity to Epcot's World Showcase by hiring youngsters aged eighteen and over to work as 'Cultural Representatives' in their nation's respective pavilions with accommodation and embarrassing uniforms – 'Costumes' in MouseSpeak – thrown in for free. The forum postings on an unofficial IP website all testified that doing the program amounted to 'the best year' of the participants' lives.

Clearly college dropouts couldn't apply for the CP. When I contacted the nearest regional recruiter, Yummy Jobs of London, I found out that, since there was no Irish pavilion in Epcot, I could forget about the IP as well. (This turned out to be a blessing in disguise because, judging by the existing member nations of the World Showcase, working in a Disneyfied Ireland would have required dressing like a leprechaun, dancing jigs on demand and greeting guests with a heartfelt 'Top of the morning to ya!' No feckin' *way*.) But Yummy Jobs were very helpful and encouraged me to apply for something called the American Cultural Resort Program instead. This would place me in a hotel or resort somewhere in the United States on an eighteen-month J-1 work visa.

I emailed a CV sometime in January 2006 and then promptly forgot all about it.

If it wasn't going to be Disney then it just wasn't for me.

We're nearly there, I swear.

Five months later I was settled into my second season in the Netherlands and halfway to my goal of drinking my own body weight in Heineken. My contract was due to end in August and I had decided not to do a third season. Instead, I planned to move to Paris where I hoped to secure a job teaching English; I had paid a deposit on a Teaching English as a Foreign Language course only the day before. ('Yeah, I'm studying in Paris,' I imagined myself telling people. 'Afterwards I'm thinking of teaching English in Vietnam.') Things were kind of slow for me and my fellow administrator Kate so we were passing the afternoon chatting, getting coffee, and periodically checking our personal email accounts.

As I logged in, I saw I had one new message from an address I didn't recognise. What in the world was the Duck and Tuna[1]? I decided it was probably spam and moved the cursor across the screen to the Delete button.

Just then, a little voice said, *'maybe this is something to do with the CV you sent to Yummy Jobs'*.

So I opened it instead.

It was from Kelly, Front Office Training Manager, thanking me for my interest in a position with them and asking me if I'd be able to participate in a telephone interview.

I closed the email and typed, 'Duck and Tuna' into

---

[1] I should point out that it was not called the Duck and Tuna, stunning and all a name as that is for a hotel. But I don't need a lawsuit right this minute, thanks.

Google.

When the results flashed up, my heart skipped a beat.

It was a resort smack bang in the middle of Walt Disney World. The Duck was one wing of the hotel, the Tuna the other. The website showcased a crescent-shaped lake, a grotto pool, quirky architecture and, in the background, the familiar golf ball-like appearance of Epcot's Spaceship Earth. Although located on Disney property, the hotels were not owned by Disney but operated by a company that for the purpose of this book we'll call International Hotels, Inc.

It sounded like the best of both worlds, not to get all Hannah Montana about it.

The interview was held at nine o'clock Dutch time the next night. I'd been up since seven that morning and at work since eight, so by the time the interview began I must have been on my eighth or ninth cup of coffee; or, in other words, only one cup away from a coronary. Luckily, on a transatlantic phone call my caffeinated giddiness was construed as 'having a good personality', and by the end of the conversation, I'd been offered the job.

Cut to Catherine screaming like a lunatic.

Back then, I was the kind of person whose spirits soared at the sight of *People* magazine on a news-stand. On a trip to New York, I was more excited at the prospect of The Gap, Victoria's Secret and Pottery Barn than I was by the Empire State Building or Central Park. Once, at the cinema, I overheard a girl behind me telling her friend that she had dual citizenship of Ireland and the US – the dream! – and I was subsequently so sick with jealousy that I didn't realise Bruce Willis was dead until someone pointed it out to me afterwards.

I remember thinking to myself that, whatever happened in Florida, it would be okay, because every morning I'd be waking up in the States. I'd have *The New York Times*, a Starbucks on every corner, the Academy

Awards shown at a more reasonable hour and – dare I hope – an annual pass to my own personal Mecca, Kennedy Space Centre.

If I had anything at all to say in my defence I would put it here, but all I have is someone to blame.

When I boarded my Orlando-bound flight that day in September, I was putting the last link in a chain that had begun over ten years before, when someone's endorsement caused me to pick up a book - the same book that opened my thirteen-year-old eyes to the idea of spending my life doing something extraordinary, or at the very least, unusual.

He had to go and put his two cents on the paperback cover of *The Hot Zone* and little me – who for all we know, was destined for a career of monotony in the insurance industry – had to go and see it. By the end of the following day - the end of the book - I was a certifiable dreamer whose head was firmly in the clouds.

Along with the rest of her.

And so, in conclusion, the blame for what follows lies at the feet of one Stephen King.

This is all his fault, in my opinion.

Two
ARRIVAL

In September 2006, the Walt Disney World Resort occupied forty-three square miles on a tract of land twice the size of Manhattan, just south of Orlando, Florida.

It boasted four theme parks, two water parks and five championship golf courses. Its nineteen themed resorts and hotels hosted an average of 100,000 guests every night and helped make Orlando one of the most popular convention destinations in the United States. It had more hotel rooms than New York City. Downtown Disney and Disney's Boardwalk conspired to keep guests from venturing into the neon and plastic that awaited them outside the gates, their outlets keeping everyone fed, watered and entertained well into the night. Events were regularly held at the 220-acre Wide World of Sports complex and Disney's Vacation Club maintained a presence with the Saratoga Springs Resort near Downtown Disney's Marketplace. A high-speed Monorail system, water taxis and a fleet of shuttle buses transported guests around the property while a dedicated fire service and security force kept them safe. At one end of World Drive was Magic Kingdom; officially the most popular theme park on the planet (and the site of the largest parking lot in the United States). At the other end of it, 20,000 people were living in the town that Disney built.

To keep all this running – and running smoothly – Disney relied on their army of 54,000 employees or 'Cast Members', and shortly after 6pm on the evening of September 5th - the day after Labor Day - they got their newest one.

Me.

The air was hot and thick as I walked out of Orlando International Airport and into my new life as a Walt Disney World Cast Member.

The hotel had sent a car to pick me up. Not only was this rather nice of them, but it helped me realise my lifelong dream of seeing someone in an Arrivals Hall holding up a sign with my name on it. In this case, the someone was Rob, a kindly grandfather type with whom I happily chatted on the short journey to the hotel.

The ride wasn't very scenic, but I was mesmerised by my first glimpse of Florida: boxy apartment buildings, vacant condominiums and monotonous mall clusters, all connected by miles and miles of unsightly power cables and framed by a bright blue sky. Every so often I even spotted the odd palm tree. I assumed we were on the outskirts of somewhere; I would spend the next eighteen months searching fruitlessly for its centre.

'Here we are,' Rob announced, after twenty minutes or so. 'Those are the gates.'

Up ahead the road ran beneath a set of purple arches, topped with multicoloured flags and a fairy-tale castle. A sign read, 'Walt Disney World: Where Dreams Come True,' while a storey-high Mickey Mouse stood to one side, welcoming me with a smile and a wave of his white glove. As we crossed onto official Disney soil, a feeling that was either excitement or airplane food-induced nausea – or perhaps both – broke over me like a wave.

I'm really here. This is actually happening.

Beyond the gates the road signs turned purple. One of them directed guests to the Epcot Resorts Area, where the Duck and Tuna was listed as one of the hotels. As made-up as it had sounded, the hotel actually did exist.

Well, that's a relief.

As we came off an exit ramp and onto Buena Vista Drive, Rob pointed out that Epcot was just beyond the trees to our right. The only thing I could see was a sign for the park's 'Backstage' entrance. After a garage of Disney's emergency vehicles and a picturesque canal, Disney-MGM's Tower of Terror suddenly loomed to our left. Across from it was my hotel.

A majestic turquoise pyramid rose into the sky, dividing a lower, rust-coloured building in two beneath it. It was flanked on either side by two enormous, um, tuna fish, striking a haughty pose with their tails in the air. In the foreground, closer to the road, a smaller, longer structure was painted the same colour but topped with two giant, um, ducks. They seemed to be ignoring the tuna fish, and each other.

By the time Rob pulled up to the doors of the Tuna wing of the hotel, I realised my face ached from smiling.

Let the magic begin.

Even if you're not an excitable, overly-emotional and jet lagged twenty-four-year-old Irish girl whose dreams are coming true, the Tuna lobby would still take your breath away.

After Rob bade me good-bye and good luck and I'd convinced the valet that I could manage one suitcase on my own, I floated in the doors on a fluffy cloud of delirium. On the other side was a small foyer whose ceiling sparkled with hundreds of tiny, twinkling stars, and beyond was the magnificent Rotunda Lobby.

Later on, I would learn all sorts of things about this space. I would know how to direct guests to the convention area, the sweet shop, the concierge, the escalators, the Disney buses, the long way to the pool, the West Elevators (located, somewhat confusingly, behind the sign for the Central Elevators). I would always show the way with a two-fingered point, because using one is considered rude in some cultures. I would come to think of this triple-height lobby as the hub, connecting the hotel's various wings and spaces, and home once a year to one of the weirdest Christmas trees you're likely to ever find on Disney property.

But for now, it was all brand new to me. I was merely a guest, seeing it for the first time and being well and truly impressed. Underneath the circus tent-like ceiling, guests were relaxing in plush armchairs lit by soft lamps, while at the lobby's apex sat a tiered fountain featuring – yes, you've guessed it – more tuna fish.

Rob had told me I'd find the front desk just inside and to the left, but now almost a quarter of the lobby was lined with different counters manned by people wearing suits and non-threatening facial expressions, and they were *all* to my left.

At the desk closest to me two burly individuals sported mint green Island Casual shirts and tended to a luggage cart; I used my best detective skills to deduce that this was the Bell Stand. At the next one over, two guys in suits stood in line with their eyes fixed on their Blackberries, while behind the counter two agents tapped quickly on unseen keyboards and stared at unseen screens. I guessed this must be the front desk and joined the queue.

When it was my turn, one of the agents – a guy about my age with short, dark hair – welcomed me to the hotel with a wide, seemingly genuine smile, and asked me if I was checking in today.

'I hope so,' I said because not yet a Front Desk Agent myself, I was unaware that this was the same lame joke cracked by approximately 83% of all guests in the Trying To Be Funny bracket.

But I *was* hoping. The sum total of my Mission Impossible instructions had been to fly to Orlando the day after Labor Day and locate my driver at Baggage Claim. It had been Rob who'd brought me to the Tuna wing; I wouldn't have known not to go to the Duck. And I wasn't sure if I'd have a normal reservation like a regular guest or if, instead, my mug shot was tacked up behind the counter with instructions to issue me the key of and directions to a disused linen closet in the basement.

Maybe that was why they needed a passport photo.

'Your name?'

I told him. There was much tapping of keys. 'Here you are. A room for fourteen nights.'

'Sure. Why not?' This comment earned me a quizzical look, so I felt compelled to add, 'I'm a J-1. I'm going to be working here.'

'Really? What department?'

'Ah, Front Desk, actually.' For some reason I felt enormously embarrassed saying this to a current Front Desk Agent.

'Wow, really?' He stuck out his hand. 'I'm Ted, the Front Office Trainer. I'll be the one training you.'

'Oh, okay.' Ted seemed disproportionately excited about this so I added a, 'Great.' Later, when I got to know him, I would come to understand that this was his genuine enthusiasm for his job and not Disney giddiness.

'You have a really nice room,' he went on, his tone conspiratorial now that we were practically colleagues. 'It has a balcony, and a view of the lake. And' – more key tapping – 'I have a letter for you, too.' He disappeared momentarily behind a partition, reappearing with a small Duck and Tuna note card. Inside was a hand-written message from someone called Caroline in 'Casting' - MouseSpeak for Human Resources - with whom I'd been exchanging emails since getting the job in May. In it, she welcomed me to the hotel, hoped my flight was okay and asked that I meet her tomorrow morning at eleven.

Handing over my room key, Ted asked if I knew when I'd be starting work.

'No idea,' I admitted. 'But apparently I'm going to Casting in the morning, so I guess I'll find out everything then.'

Up on the fifth floor, my room did indeed have a balcony.

Unfortunately it also faced directly onto another wing of the hotel, i.e. a wall, but if I turned to the left I could see a slice of the lake, the lap pool at the Duck and the Tower of Terror – a 'partial lake view' in high-priced hotel language. But I could hardly complain, seeing as it was free and I'd only be complaining to my future department.

After I unpacked a few things, tried out the bed (heavenly!) and flipped through the TV channels, I grabbed some dollars and set off to explore. I managed to find the lobby again – on Level 3, just to shake things up – and in it, the gift shop.

As I'm physically incapable of passing by a good gift shop, I stopped inside to have a look. The smiling sales assistants wore lanyards adorned with colourful Disney trading pins and the same *you can approach me, I'll help you* expressions as everyone else. I admired the Cinderella music boxes, the Minnie plush toys and the Disney World 2006 apparel. One corner of the store was filled with all things shaped like Mickey's head: plates, cushions, oven gloves, novelty straws, photo frames, watch faces and – insert your own joke here – mouse pads.

I left with just a copy of *People* magazine which was more than enough excitement for me.

I knew from my obsessive stalking of the hotel's website that the two wings were connected by a palm tree-lined walkway that stretched across an inlet of the manmade lake. Opposite the front desk escalators led down to ground level, so I hoped for the best and headed that way.

In the minute it took me to walk from the gift shop to the rear doors, I passed by two elevator banks, a sweet shop, a piano, a coffee bar, a spa and three restaurants – four if you counted the one in the corner I could see but didn't technically pass. The sheer size of the complex was overwhelming. Combined, the hotel boasted 2,265 guest rooms, eight restaurants, two cafes, five separate swimming pools with two pool-side eateries, a white sand lakeside beach, two gyms, a spa, two business centres, a twenty-four-hour convenience store and over 300,000 feet of dedicated convention space.

Orientation was going to take *forever*.

Having located the doors, I walked outside into the Orlando evening and one of the most stunning manmade vistas I had ever seen.

The waters of the lake were still, a perfect reflection of the hotel's idiosyncratic design shimmering on its surface. This mirror image was interrupted only by the walkway, lined with luscious palms and decorated with colourful flower beds. I walked halfway across before turning to look back at the five-tiered fountain of upturned shells that sat at the pyramid's base, the largest one held aloft by the tails of four two-dimensional tuna fish while the water poured into a pond below.

At the other end of the walkway I noticed, in the distance, a sign made entirely of light bulbs directing guests towards Disney's Boardwalk. The only person I had ever met who had worked in Disney World was a girl called Claire whom I knew from my time with Holidaybreak. She had been on the International Program, stationed at the UK pavilion, and had told me that one of her favourite Disney places was a duelling piano bar called Jellyrolls. I was pretty sure she had said it was on the Boardwalk, so I headed that way.

You probably won't be shocked to learn that the Boardwalk, as the name suggests, is an actual boardwalk that sits on the shores of Crescent Lake. It's opposite Disney's Yacht and Beach Clubs and all three complexes have white clapboard facades reminiscent of an Atlantic Coast seaside resort. Shops, restaurants and bars crowd the Boardwalk's promenade amid twinkling fairy lights, flashing neon signage and piped jazz musak. At the far end a bridge leads to Epcot's International Gateway entrance which deposits guests somewhere between the UK pavilion's red telephone boxes and France's miniature *La Tour Eiffel*. Disney water-taxis – the 'Friendships', if you can keep your dinner down – ferry guests to and fro.

As I stood there, the Boardwalk seemed to enjoy a quiet, relaxed calm. There were no long lines, life-sized cartoon characters, or squabbling children. As the promenade's twinkling lights drizzled onto the lake below, the musak played and boxes of salt water taffy sat in store windows, I found myself nostalgic for a place I'd never been and wistful for a simpler time which I was far too young to remember.

I loved it.

I passed the Atlantic Dance Hall, as much of a nightclub as the Boardwalk's theme would allow (although, in the months that followed, the only people I ever saw doing any kind of Atlantic dance were the unfortunate Cast Members who manned the doors; they seemed contractually obligated to dance whilst on duty). Next to it was the famed Jellyrolls, silent and dark; a sign promised it would be opening shortly. When I came upon the Big River Grille and got a whiff of hot food, it suddenly occurred to me that somewhere beneath all this excitement, I was totally starving.

'Only you?' the hostess asked, unable to keep the surprise out of her voice. Lone diners were apparently a rare sight in these parts. I took a table outside with an unobstructed view of the promenade and the lake beyond it, ordering a Coke because I was thirsty and a cocktail because I was celebrating.

Smiling inside and out, I was struggling to process all that was happening. Was I really here? Was I actually in Disney World?

By the time I had finished my burger and ordered a second cocktail for dessert, it was almost nine o'clock. With Florida lagging five hours behind Ireland, my body was under the impression it was almost two in the morning, and I'd been up since five. *People* magazine's celebrity cellulite photos were beginning to blur before my eyes and so, with my comfy bed beckoning, I asked for the check.

Suddenly there was a loud *pop* and a blossom of gold unfurled in the sky. My waitress informed me that it was Illumi-NATIONS, the laser show and fireworks display that closed nearby Epcot each evening. For the next twenty-five minutes I sat open-mouthed as each batch of pyrotechnics outdid the one before, until the finale filled the sky with simultaneous explosions of colour and light and sparkle.

I left with my dinner bill and a massive lump in my throat. There was magic in these moments. Not long ago, I'd been stuck in Cork with a future so bleak I couldn't bear to look at it, but now it was as beautiful and bright as a night sky full of Disney fireworks.

I had clearly inhaled my first batch of pixie dust and I was *loving* it.

And I hadn't seen anything yet; I'd barely left the grounds of the hotel. On the walk back, I stood and looked at the Tuna from its left side - four fingers stretching out into the lake, illuminated cup-shaped fountains atop each one. In the daylight it was a stunning palace surreal against the sky but at night, words failed.

I leaned on the railing and took it in, or tried to. I wasn't sure what I'd done to deserve coming to a place like this, but it must have been something pretty good. This morning I'd woken up in dull, dreary Ireland, only to have my Disney dream delivered to me by the end of the day.

Standing at the foot of the hotel that night, I was probably as happy as I'd ever been.

I had no idea that in a few short hours, my Disney bubble would be well and truly burst.

Three
MOUSETRAPPED

The next morning, and after a breakfast of thirty-dollar Mickey Mouse-shaped chocolate chip pancakes and a flip through my complimentary copy of *USA Today*, I made my way to the basement of the hotel, home of the Casting Department, where I found Caroline sitting at her desk.

'Hi,' I said as brightly as I could muster midmorning, 'I'm Catherine.' I just about resisted the urge to add, 'I'm he-ere!'

I allowed Caroline a moment to compose herself, thinking she was about to come at me with outstretched arms while the trumpets, ticker tape shower and party poppers began. I had, after all, just travelled half way around the world to take up employment with these people; surely there would be some sort of welcome ceremony to mark my arrival. But Caroline just smiled and asked me to have a seat.

Maybe, I thought, *she just wants to get the formalities out of the way before the party starts.*

Presently another Casting person – or was it Casting Agent? – emerged from behind a partition and motioned for me to go and join her back there. This 'Michelle' individual then proceeded to interview me for the job I already had, as if I'd just walked in off the street that minute. If I'd known that was going to happen, I might have worn something other than my 'Love Stinks' T-shirt (complete with cartoon skunk) and I definitely would have tied back my humidity-challenged hair.

I watched with silent dismay as Michelle circled 'Fair' next to Appearance on her interview checklist.

Fifteen minutes' worth of questions later, I was sent back out to the main office. Perhaps now all that was out of the way, Caroline would give me a hug, apologise and take me out for Starbucks or something. But instead she sat me at a computer terminal and had me fill out a twenty page online form ('for Corporate'), after which she announced it was time for my mandatory drugs test.

These people could really do with some professional help in planning their welcome parties.

I was escorted back up to the entrance where I was then bundled into a Lincoln Town Car and driven to an undisclosed location somewhere in the vicinity of Sea World. I tried to take mental pictures of the sights we passed en route (an outlet mall, Dolly Parton's Dixie Stampede, a steak house that looked like a movie theatre) just in case I'd later be recalling this journey for the authorities.

The medical practice where the testing was to take place was a nondescript storefront office in a building of equally nondescript storefront offices, all off-white walls and dirty blinds. It would have been the perfect place for an abortionist or bail bondsman to set up shop. I left my driver with his Christian radio and took a seat in the waiting room, silently praying I'd be able to pee on demand.

Having never been screened for drugs before, I was nervous. Just like the illogical thoughts that manifest themselves whenever a security guard seems to be walking towards you – you know you haven't done anything, but you begin to wonder – I feared I had somehow managed to accidentally ingest illegal drugs despite my efforts to stay at least ten feet away from anything that could possibly be considered an illegal substance, however remote the chance. Subsequently I hadn't picked up as much as a Magic Marker in over four months.

But then there was all that Xanax I popped on the plane yesterday...

When my turn came, the lab technician – a squat, dark-haired man with a thick Eastern European accent – eyed me with suspicion as I secured my purse in a locker. He handed me a small plastic cup and a pair of latex gloves, directed me to a bathroom, and locked me inside.

Bright yellow tape emblazoned with, 'DO NOT TOUCH' was wrapped around the sink, taps and toilet handle, and almost everywhere was covered with a layer of clear plastic. It looked like the world's cleanest crime scene.

Feeling very *CSI*, I pulled on the gloves and unscrewed the cup's cap. I'll spare you the details, but it was surprisingly easy to do on target – men must actually be *trying* to coat the entire toilet seat – and when I was done I gave a firm knock on the door, indicating that I was ready to be relived, no pun intended, of my plastic cup.

Mr Lab Tech took the cup in his gloved hands, checked the lid was secure, and then held it up to the light, studying it. Now, I didn't really know enough about drug screening to argue, but I had my doubts that this was standard procedure.

Then he said, 'You did not tell me you were pregnant.'

What...?

For a beat, the world ceased to spin on its axis, the air became still, the only sound that of blood rushing in my ears. I momentarily forgot that (a) my being pregnant was a biological impossibility unless I had been unwittingly chosen for the lead role in *The Immaculate Conception II: The Atheist* and (b) the medical community had not yet, to my knowledge, devised a way to determine pregnancy by assessing the colour of a woman's urine.

But a moment feels like a long time when a member of the medical community – however tenuous that membership may be – tells you that you are pregnant, especially when that wasn't even the question you asked.

'I'm not pregnant,' I said hopefully.

'I just make joke!' Lab Tech said, his face breaking into a huge, toothy grin. 'I say same thing to all the ladies! I tell them all they pregnant! Good one, no? It's funny. What? You don't agree?'

Back at the hotel and thankfully, not impregnated, I found Caroline at her desk and writing my name on a little green card.

'This is your staff cafeteria pass,' she said, handing it over. 'You can eat three meals a day there while you're staying here at the hotel.'

I mumbled thanks and tried to look grateful, but I very much doubted that they were serving Mickey Mouse-shaped pancakes in *there*.

'If you need any help finding an apartment, let me know,' she went on. 'I have a few telephone numbers I can give you.'

'That'd be great, thanks.'

'And we have to wait ten days before you can apply for your Social Security Number, so...' She consulted a desk calendar. 'Come back and see me on Friday.'

'This Friday? Like, the day after tomorrow?'

'No, next Friday. Ten days from now.'

'But...when do I start work?'

'You can't start work until you have your Social,' she said, leaving the word *obviously* unspoken at the end of the sentence.

'So, in two weeks?'

'No.' Caroline looked confused by my confusion. 'You can't apply for it for another ten days and then it can take up to six to eight weeks for the number to come through.'

'Oh.'

I had had a vague notion that I would be starting work within a few days of my arrival, but where had I got that idea? I quickly did a mental inventory of all correspondence between myself and the hotel, but couldn't pinpoint exactly where I'd picked that up. But then I was fairly certain that if anyone had mentioned a two-month delay, I'd remember it – that was, after all, the kind of detail that stuck in your mind. Now I might have to go for eight weeks without a pay-check? My mind ran frantically through my finances and came back with a Code Red.

I took a deep breath. There was no need to panic.

'Is there any chance it'll come through sooner?' I asked.

'Oh, sure,' Caroline said, absently shuffling papers on her desk. 'There's always a chance.'

I told myself that this was not a disaster. Tsunamis, earthquakes, the AIDS epidemic – *those* were disasters. This wasn't even a hiccup in the larger scheme of things. And I did have a free room in a fabulous hotel in Walt Disney World. Okay, so I didn't have the money to actually go *into* any of the parks, but there were still plenty of other things to do instead.

Weren't there?

By Friday lunchtime – forty-eight hours later – I'd exhausted most of my recreational options. Thursday morning I'd sat on my balcony with a coffee and a book. On Thursday afternoon, I'd sat by the pool with a Coke and a book. On Thursday night, I'd sat on the Boardwalk with a coffee and a sandwich, because I was hungry and because I'd finished my book.

So I was excited to be heading out, 'off property'.

My cousin Aisling happened to be on holiday in

Orlando at the time, and we had arranged to meet up at her hotel on Friday afternoon. I could barely contain myself at the thought of seeing somewhere other than Epcot Resorts, and talking to someone who wasn't serving me food at the same time. I vowed that I and the credit card my parents had given me for emergencies would make the most of our time outside the Disney gates.

I was desperately in need of reading material and a hairdryer, so I hatched a cunning plan. I decided I'd take a taxi first to Florida Mall, from where – after a couple of hours of, ahem, window shopping – I'd take another cab to Aisling's hotel, the Universal Crowne Plaza. According to my Avis road map of Orlando, both locations were quite close together. Only inches apart, in fact.

I left my hotel just after lunch. All morning the sun had been shining but as soon as my Town Car drove beyond the gates, a giant thundercloud appeared above us, looking not unlike the alien mothership from *Independence Day*. It then proceeded to unleash meteorological hell. The car was hammered with thick sheets of drenching rain, obscuring any view I might hope to have had of the greater Orlando area. The sky cracked with thunder and lightning, visibility was almost nil but not once did my driver slow to below sixty.

When we reached Florida Mall, I ran from the cab to the door. In the two or three seconds it took to do that, the ends of my jeans still managed to soak up an entire puddle which then leaked slowly back into my shoes for the next hour.

The Florida Mall is a popular shopping spot with tourists and locals alike, a home to all major brands (The Gap! Victoria's Secret! Banana Republic!) as well as a couple of department stores, a food court and not one, but two Starbucks outlets. The mall is also connected to the lobby of the Florida Hotel, voted the Number One Hotel in the World by *Shopaholics' Quarterly*. (Okay, so I made that up, but if such a thing *did* exist, wouldn't it win it?) It also boasts the world's largest M&M store, although I'm not entirely sure that's anything to boast about.

I picked up a hairdryer and a pair of straighteners in JC Penney's electrical department, then hit Walden Books for some literary sustenance. Curtis Sittenfeld's *Prep* was practically shrieking at me from a shelf just inside the door, so I grabbed it and made for the cashier, justifying my purchase with the favourable US Dollar/Euro exchange rate. But then I wondered when I might be in a bookstore again, so I picked up another two books, three magazines and a pretty notebook, just in case things got so bad that I had to start writing my own reading material.

After the requisite Starbucks stop, I hailed a taxi and made my way to Aisling's hotel. I had no idea what part of Orlando I was in – or even if this was still Orlando – but wherever it was, it looked like The Town That Town Planning Forgot.

Nothing was more than a storey high or not shaped like a box. The unifying theme seemed to be the juxtaposition of overhead power lines and traffic lights. I passed a tacky gift shop, a parked helicopter, pirate-themed miniature golf, a water park, an upside-down museum, a movie theatre, a Hooters, a British pub and a branch of every fast-food restaurant known to man. Hordes of dazed, sunburned tourists were drifting into these places like zombies, wallets open, credit cards out.

Aisling and I hung out at the hotel for a while before moving to a place nearby called O'Shucks, a storefront bar with sad shamrocks in the windows and sawdust on the floor - O'Shucks indeed. But karaoke was scheduled to start at nine and there was a special on pitchers of Bud Lite, so we found a seat and ordered our first. I was chuffed to be asked for ID, not realising that I would have to produce it every time I wanted as much as an R-rated movie ticket for the next year and a half.

It was past three in the morning before I returned to the Tuna. Utterly sober at the bar, my condition had deteriorated somewhat in the cab on the way back. I shushed myself as my shoes clacked loudly across the lobby's tiled floor, earning me a questioning look from the lone Cast Member vacuuming near the elevators.

I fell into bed fully clothed and waited for the room to stop spinning so I could close my eyes and sleep. It had been nice to get out of Disney for a while, nice to see Aisling, nice to relax with a few beers.

But it was also nice to be back in the safe arms of the Mouse, back inside the manicured lawns and pleasing aesthetics of the place where they said magic lived.

The real world, with its tack and its neon and its plastic, could stay outside.

Four
APARTMENT LIVING

As my second week in Orlando drew to a close, I dragged myself away from my hectic schedule of sunbathing, reading and being monumentally bored, and started thinking about where exactly I was going to live for the next year and a half.

This was no easy task. My only sense of the city and its surrounds was my Avis road map and, with no transportation, driving licence or friends to ask for advice, I didn't even know where to begin, or how. Casting Caroline hadn't been much help either; she'd given me the telephone number of some guy who rented rooms (and who, she claimed, 'a lot of J-1s' used) and nodded in the direction of a stack of *Apartment Finder* magazines. I figured that renting a room, as opposed to renting an apartment, was my only option, as without a Social Security Number, a bank account or a job I could barely rent a bicycle, let alone sign a lease. So with homelessness imminent, I placed a call to this Some Guy.

His name was James. Although apathetic and disinterested in the trials and tribulations of my Orlando life, he did have good news: an en-suite master bedroom was available in nearby Plantation Park.

According to the all-knowing Internet, Plantation

Park was a gated complex on Vineland Avenue, about a mile from the Mouse. Theoretically I could walk from there into work along State Road 535, as well as to a Publix Supermarket and the Premium Outlet Mall, and so be fed and clothed. Not only was living within walking distance of anything pretty rare in Orlando but rumour had it that these routes even had sidewalks as well. In such an anti-pedestrian autotopia, this was nothing short of miraculous.

On the developer's website I studied the floor plans and artistic renderings as if they were crime scene photos and the outcome of this case was going to make or break my entire criminal justice career. There was a large swimming pool (still a novelty this early in), a twenty-four hour gym in case motivation struck for the first time in twenty-four years, and a clubhouse whose interior could have come straight out of a Pottery Barn catalogue, and probably did.

The cost was $600 a month including utilities. In addition to my first month's rent, I also had to pay a security deposit of $350. To put these amounts in perspective, I was going to earn around $1,200 a month and, right now, I had no idea when I was going to start earning it.

But I had no choice. I needed to check out of the hotel and I needed to live in a place where I could walk back to it. And it was certainly better than the alternative: living out of my suitcase in the shelter of a freeway overpass.

So I told James I'd take it and thus my fate was sealed.

James and I had had three telephone conversations before I moved in, during which he told me that at present, the apartment was occupied by one guy who was due to move out before I'd arrive. There could, sometime in the future, be up to four other people living in the two other bedrooms and sharing the living space with me, but for now at least, I'd have the place to myself. The unit was fully furnished with bed linen and towels provided, and the kitchen was equipped for all sorts of culinary adventures. James gently dissuaded me from viewing the place before I moved in, claiming he couldn't show it until the current occupant had left, and his departure practically overlapped with my arrival, leaving inadequate time in between for a grand tour.

(ALARM BELLS! ALARM BELLS! ALARM BELLS!)

But I was at ease with my decision. The complex looked great, the location was perfect, and James didn't sound like a kidney thief.

What was the worst that could happen?

I decided to move my stuff in on Monday 18th September, then go back and stay at the hotel for one last night. James promised to meet me outside Plantation Park's clubhouse at one o'clock, but it was forty-five minutes after that when he arrived. Although I didn't think he could be older than thirty, he already looked middle-aged with both his waistline and hairline headed in the wrong direction. He heaved my suitcase into the back seat of his car and drove us the fifty feet to my new home.

The first sign that something was awry was his casual mention that two girls were already living in the apartment.

'But they'll be moving out soon,' he added quickly.

Either they had the shortest rental agreement in history or this was a different apartment to the one I'd been promised.

Well, there goes my plan to spend the foreseeable future pottering around in my pyjamas.

The apartment was on the ground floor of a building near the entrance, within sight of the tennis court and mailboxes. James knocked but got no answer. After a second one failed to rouse a response, he started to dig in his pockets for a key. But then there came a scurrying sound from somewhere inside and moments later a tiny, dark-haired girl who looked to be about twelve (but who was actually eighteen, I'd later learn, and from Kazakhstan) slowly opened the door.

'James!' she said, a little louder than I thought was really necessary.

As she stood to one side so we could enter, I noticed that there was an inordinately large collection of shoes lined up against the wall behind her. There must have been ten pairs and at least five different sizes.

A short hallway led to two of the three bedrooms, and from this darkened corner emerged the second girl. She looked very much like the first but taller, dressed only in a bath towel and apparently mute. She gave a little wave.

With another step the living room came into view, as did the two guys sprawled casually across its only furniture: a large couch of indeterminable colour and a coffee table that had been tortured with hot cups. They looked decidedly bemused by my arrival.

The kitchen, separated from the living room by a breakfast bar, had all the basics, or at least it looked like it might somewhere beneath the piles of encrusted dishes, scattered crumbs and empty food cartons. I counted seven pizza boxes on the floor by the trashcan.

Two hastily-rolled sleeping bags were slung on top of the dryer.

My bedroom was next on the tour although now I wasn't so sure I wanted to see it. I followed James through the door off the living room and into a large, square room. It had both the promised en-suite bathroom and enormous walk-in closet but what it didn't have was much of anything else.

There was a bare twin mattress sagging on a box spring and pushed into a corner next to a misassembled chest of drawers. Through the open bathroom door I could see yellowing tiles claiming to have once been white. A used bar of soap was stuck to the sink, complete with dark curly hairs of an unknown origin. A naked bulb hung from the ceiling below a fan whose blades were furry with dust; the switch on the wall activated neither.

Out of the corner of my eye I saw James watching me.

'It's fine,' I said weakly.

But it wasn't, and neither was I. I was feeling sick. My naiveté rose up and smacked me in the face like a garden shovel I'd accidentally stepped on. It wasn't that the photos online had lied, or even that James had. I just hadn't been expecting *this*.

Yes, it was spacious and I suspected that should the living room blinds ever be opened, the space would fill with natural light. But with so little furniture, right now it looked like an abandoned office from the Eighties, right down to the dusty Venetian blinds and fluorescent lighting.

To summarise, my new home had all the charm of a French public toilet. And I don't mean one of those flashy Parisian ones with the electronic door – I mean the kind you find by the beach that consists of a hole in the floor and an invitation to squat.

I resisted the urge to succumb to hysterics while James outlined the details of the twelve-month lease. I handed over almost all the money I had in the world, signed my name and ignored the audience out in the living room who watched the proceedings through the open door, whispering amongst themselves and giggling.

James told me that it was my responsibility to report any 'extra' people living in the apartment. That was when I realised powers of observation weren't exactly his strong point.

After he left I ventured into the living room and attempted to make small talk. The girls just looked at me blankly while the guys – their boyfriends, I was not shocked to discover, and also from Kazakhstan – had at least some grasp of the English language.

'You from Ireland!' one of them exclaimed on learning of my superlative nationality. 'You like to drink, no? Guinness, yes? You drink Guinness?' He said this with the sort of admiration one normally reserves for Pulitzer Prize winners, Olympic gold medalists and Nobel Laureates.

Before I could respond, two more girls wandered into the living room followed by another guy, this one younger again and sporting a head of dark curly hair.

'Hi,' I said, 'I'm Catherine.' *I believe you've been using my bathroom..?*

'We hide,' Curly-Haired Guy said. All three of the newcomers stared at me, awaiting a reaction. 'From James,' he clarified. 'We hide from James.'

I wasn't too sure I wanted to know, but I had to ask. 'You live here too?'

Everyone looked towards Curly-Haired, evidently the elected spokesperson. 'Oh, no,' he said, shaking his head. Then, 'Yes.'

'You do or you don't?'

'What?'

'Live here.'

'How long you came here?' he said, ignoring my question.

'I arrived two weeks ago.'

'No.' He rolled his eyes, exasperated. 'How long you *came* here?'

Several different ways of saying it later, I realised he wanted to know how long I was going to be living in Orlando.

'A year and a half,' I said.

'A year and a half!' He was incredulous. 'You get work visa?'

I nodded. 'I'll be working in Disney World.'

This seemed to mildly impress him, even though at least every other person around here worked there too. 'I work at Hilton,' he said. 'Housekeeping.' He jerked a thumb in the direction of the other girls, hovering by the breakfast bar. 'They work in Pizza Hut.'

Well that explains the pizza boxes.

'But finish now,' he continued. 'We leave twenty-fifth.'

'Twenty-fifth of this month – like, September?'

'Yes, twenty-fifth.' He face broke into a grin. 'Ticket to Miami!'

I gestured at the other six strangers scattered around my new living room. 'All of you? All of you leave on the twenty-fifth?'

'Twenty-fifth, yes.' He made a thumbs-up sign. 'Ticket to Miami!'

Having clearly breached the limits of our capacity to communicate, I left all seven of my possible apartment-mates and retreated to my room, where I sat on the bare mattress, reviewed the situation and tried not to cry.

When I'd first arrived in Florida two weeks ago, the world was a much happier place. So okay, Caroline hadn't been as excited to see me as her exclamation mark-riddled emails might have implied, and she had somehow neglected to mention that it could be two months before I started work, but that wasn't the end of the world. Being stuck in Disney with no funds, friends or transport hadn't exactly been a picnic, but there were people who paid vast sums of money to spend a fortnight lying by a pool in the sun. And I had had something to look forward to: moving into my new Orlando apartment, where I could get settled and comfortably while away the time until I had a job to go to or friends to see.

But now I found myself the only non-Russian speaker in a depressing yet expensive squatters' den. It was anyone's guess how many people I was actually sharing the place with – or, for that matter, *who* I was sharing it with – and I couldn't lock my bedroom door from either side. The last shreds of positivity I'd been clinging to for the past fortnight seeped out of me and I was left feeling utterly deflated.

I had planned to spend the afternoon happily unpacking but now the dirty white walls started to close in on me. So I grabbed my key, told my Kazak friends I'd see them tomorrow – cue seven blank stares – and headed back to the secure comfort of my hotel room, where I'd spend the night lying awake in the dark, trying to recall all the good reasons I had for coming to Orlando in the first place.

First thing the next morning, it was off to nearby Kissimmee to apply for my Social Security Number, the magic digits that would unlock the door to paid employment. Outside, the ground baked in white-hot heat and swarms of little black fornicating 'love bugs' descended on anything stationary.

I was back at Plantation Park by lunchtime, and happy to see things were looking somewhat cleaner. Although the front door was unlocked – I walked straight on in to an empty apartment – the dishes had been washed and put away, the trash removed and the carpet vacuumed. My bathroom, thankfully, was now free of pubic hairs and almost toxic with the smell of bleach.

I put on some music and began the sad process of unpacking. I removed the plastic wrap from my bed linen – Wal-Mart's finest – and made up the bed with the thin sheets, starchy comforter and wafer thin pillow; I'd had thicker slices of toast. Then I sat on it with my back against the wall and had an innocent search with my laptop for any unsecured wireless networks that might be lurking in the air nearby.

I had only been sitting there for a minute or two when the exterior wall I was leaning against shuddered violently. I sat up with a start and the shaking ceased.

That was kind of weird.

With everything still once again I went back to my computer, only to have the very same thing happen again not five minutes later. Either Florida was suddenly on a fault line or a T-Rex was wandering around outside.

Then it clicked.

On the other side of the wall, a metal staircase was affixed to the building, taking people up to the first floor. Apparently every time someone walked up them the wall – its constituents mainly plasterboard and air – shook with every step.

I moved the bed to the opposite wall to avoid the tremors and, in doing so, revealed an electric cord lying on the floor. One end was plugged into a socket and on the other end was a button. I looked around to see if there was any likely candidate for what it controlled, but could find nothing.

So out of curiosity, I pushed it.

A wailing siren, pulsating from all angles and audible, surely, throughout the entire complex, began before the button had even come back up. I clapped my hands over my ears and ran out into the living room where my room-mates (one official, one non-official) were doing the same thing.

'What is that?' Curly-Haired shouted over the din. Tall Mute Girl pulled open the cover on the alarm system's keypad and began frantically pressing buttons.

I shook my head, feigning ignorance. It would take half an hour to explain that I had unwittingly pressed what had turned out to be a panic button, and what difference would it make anyway? We still had to figure out how to turn the damn thing off.

Curly-Haired took off running towards the clubhouse, while Tall Mute Girl and I sat on the couch with our hands over our ears. More than five minutes passed before a complex rent-a-cop arrived at a slow gait, pressed a button on the key pad and sauntered off.

Blissful quiet was back but somewhere towards the rear of my mind, near long division and the Christian names of all the New Kids, a little voice asked, 'Catherine, why does your room have a panic button?'

Later, my first night in Plantation Park proved sleepless.

Not only were my Kazak friends having a social gathering on the other side of my door, but the air conditioning unit for the entire building was right outside my window and barely four feet from my head. Every twenty minutes or so it whirred into action, yanking me out of the light sleep I'd just managed to slip into only moments before. At one point, this mechanical sound was joined by another, a sort of repetitive clapping, as if something was hitting the rotating blades of the fan. Sure enough, come the morning, the mangled body of a black snake lay across the top of the unit.

Lovely.

It was nearly eleven before I managed to drag myself out of bed. After a furtive sweep of the living room determined that no one else was home, I ventured out to make a cup of coffee. Task completed and with still no sign of anyone else, I plonked myself on the couch–of–questionable-cleanliness and turned on CNN.

Okay, the Discovery Channel.

All right, it was *The Hills*. Happy now?

Anyway, a short time later, the front door opened and a man I'd never seen before strode into the apartment. Apparently he hadn't expected to find me on the couch, because he stopped in his tracks when he saw me.

'Sorry,' he said. 'I think I've got the wrong apartment.'

'I think you do.'

We stared at each other for another moment before he turned on his heel and left. I released the breath I hadn't known I'd been holding, ran to the door and bolted it shut behind him.

That night I told the others in my best authoritative voice that the front door had to be kept locked at all times. I wasn't sure they grasped the concept, but I started locking it myself in the hope they'd catch on. And before I went to sleep each night, I dragged the chest of drawers in front of my bedroom door and moved the bed back to the other wall, within easy reach of the panic button.

For the next seven days, all my apartment-mates saw of me was the path I tread from my bedroom to the front door first thing each morning and back again that night.

I had discovered Downtown Disney, a mile-long shopping, dining and entertainment development only a short stroll from my local Disney gates and the perfect place for me to kill a few hours, or an entire day. (While incarcerated at the Tuna I hadn't realised you didn't need an admission ticket to get in and therefore never went.)

Each morning I'd shower and dress before starting the forty-minute walk to Downtown Disney, where I'd arrive desperately needing to shower again. The average daily temperature soared to a suffocating ninety degrees and I began to see giant ice-cold Cokes sweating condensation a few steps ahead on the sidewalk, taunting me with their bendy straws.

My adventures would begin at Marketplace, home to the world's largest Disney merchandise store, World of Disney. I might have a look at their scrap-booking supplies, or grab an ice cream at Ghirardelli, although usually the first thing I did was run to the restrooms to check just how much I resembled a tomato. Beyond that was Pleasure Island (PI), a cluster of themed nightclubs that Disney hoped would stop its guests from seeking out clubs off property, and an Irish bar and restaurant called Raglan Road. PI was as lively as a graveyard until night fell, but I occasionally sat at Raglan's bar mid-afternoon to have a Heineken, if I was treating myself.

But my favourite playground was Westside, the jewel in Downtown Disney's commercial crown. It had a Planet Hollywood, a House of Blues, a five-storey arcade called Disney Quest and was home to *La Nouba*, a Cirque du Soleil production. I spent my time in the gigantic Virgin Megastore and the AMC movie theatre beside it. I'd begin by perusing the shelves of Virgin's book and magazine section, a treasure trove of unusual and quirky titles, and if I was having a bad self-control day, I might even buy something. After a latte in the store's cafe (conveniently located right next to the book section), I'd make my way over to AMC and watch a movie.

Or two.

(Sly wink).

Then as the sun began its journey back down the other side of the sky, I'd start off home along 535, an ugly slice of Strip Mall USA whose traffic was kept consistently bumper-to-bumper by its I-4 exit ramp. For the evening I'd retreat to my room to read or write and once the racket in the living room had subsided, I'd turn off the lights and spend another night awake in the dark.

I kept conversations with the Kazaks to a minimum. At first they'd treated me like the new, shiny toy, trying to engage me in conversation as I made coffee in the kitchen or loaded my laundry into the machine, and there had been one very strange incident in which Tall Mute Girl had knocked on my bedroom door and invited me, by way of hand signals, to join her for a session at the gym. (I had politely declined.) But they soon got the message that I was just waiting for them to leave and stopped inviting me to their living room soirees, which seemed to be getting louder and longer each night.

Then one morning, in the second week of our co-habitation, I awoke to an eerie silence. Even the air conditioning, it seemed, was quiet. With considerable trepidation, I pulled open my bedroom door and was met with a strange and yet wonderful sight.

The living room was spotlessly clean. Every surface in the kitchen was newly reflective and there were no piles of pizza boxes or mountains of wet clothes. I checked the fridge and found only my lonely carton of coffee creamer and a tub of cream cheese. All the other cabinets were empty. The other two bedrooms were bare and two sets of keys lay on the breakfast bar.

A slow smile spread across my face as it dawned on

me that today was the twenty-fifth, AKA Ticket To Miami Day. The torment was over.

At least for the moment, anyway. It was anyone's guess what strange creatures I'd be forced to cohabit with next, but for now I could bask in the glory of having the entire apartment to myself.

The Kazaks had insisted on pushing the couch against the living room's back wall, making it appear even more stark and uninviting than it already was. Now I pulled it out a few feet and centred the coffee table. If you closed the blinds, only left the kitchen light on and squinted, you could almost convince yourself the place was cosy.

I put some clothes in the washing machine. I spread my paltry collection of foodstuffs around the kitchen with reckless abandon. I threw my bedroom door open and dead-bolted the front door instead.

I ordered some pizza online, brought my pillow and blanket out from my room and settled on the couch for a resplendent evening of *Grey's Anatomy*, barbecue chicken pizza and the most delicious, exquisite solitude.

A week later I was settled in for another night of gorgeous doctors and clogged arteries when there came a knock at the door.

Outside in the dark stood two of the Kazak girls, the one who had opened the door to James and I the day I arrived, and Tall Mute Girl. They were wearing lots of make-up and dressed for a night on a street corner; a combined harvest of both their outfits wouldn't have yielded enough material for a cushion cover.

Weren't they supposed to be in Miami?

'Hello Cathy!' the non-mute one said, all smiles, as if I were a dear friend they hadn't seen in ages. And for the record, I despise being called Cathy.

'Did you forget something?' I asked, skipping the pleasantries. *Grey's* was starting in less than five minutes and I had been planning on never seeing these people again.

They shook their heads, *no*. They looked at each other, then back at me. Tall Mute Girl poked the other one in the ribs, prompting her to take a breath and begin to speak.

'We need favour,' she began.

Using mostly nouns, she then explained that instead of heading south, they had decided to outstay their visa and remain in the States illegally. Since complexes like Plantation Park operated a strict system - keeping copies of your passport and visa documentation on file as long as you were a resident - they had no choice but to move in with a family in Kissimmee who were willing to turn a blind eye in exchange for the rent paid in cash. Of course, this new arrangement had curtailed their all-night gatherings, but today was someone's birthday, and they were just wondering...

Since I stayed in my room all the time anyway, could they possibly throw a party in the living room?

'You come too, if you like,' she added generously.

I took a moment to admire their sheer audacity before I slammed the door shut in their hopeful little faces.

Five
ORIENTATION

Despite Caroline's foreboding, my Social Security Number arrived at the hotel a mere seven days after I applied for it.

I was in the midst of a pleasant mid-afternoon stroll through Downtown Disney when my new cell phone buzzed with a call from Casting; they wanted to sign me up for an Orientation class in just two days' time. I had been suffering through thoughts of the worst possible outcome but now had lucked out with the best.

I was going to start work just three weeks and a day after arriving in Florida.

Orientation was scheduled to start at nine on Wednesday morning in something called the Learning Centre.

Not wanting to walk for forty minutes in corduroy trousers – the only professional-looking garment I had in my possession – I took a cab to the hotel. As soon as it came to a stop in the hotel's parking lot, I flung a twenty-dollar bill into the front seat and ran from the vehicle as if it were engulfed in flames, lest any of my soon-to-be colleagues caught sight of me taking a taxi to work.

The service entrance was around the side of the hotel and down a hill. Caroline had instructed me to walk right in the door, go past Security and into the Learning Centre, which she promised would be the next open door on the left. Somehow I managed to miss the Cast Entrance – despite the big sign saying WELCOME WORLD'S GREATEST CAST - and in my subsequent fluster, walked in through a swinging door on the loading dock, despite the big sign saying DO NOT ENTER BY THIS DOOR.

After a good five minutes of wandering through the myriad of 'backstage' corridors, each one utterly indistinguishable from the next, I finally located the famous Learning Centre, which turned out to be a small meeting room with a projection screen, some white boards and a fresh batch of trainees sat around several small tables. At the one closest to the door was a blonde girl about my age, and when she flashed a friendly smile I took a seat next to her. She was Sara, she told me, from Iowa, and she would soon be working for Camp Tuna, the hotel's baby-sitting service. I tried not to look surprised when she told me that she was married at just twenty-one; if all Americans were getting married so young, then that might go some way to explain the country's astronomical divorce rate.

Shortly after nine, Charlie from Casting flounced in the door with a smile that wouldn't leave her face once for the next two days. She was clearly ecstatic to be working at the Duck and Tuna and her enthusiasm was infectious. As she talked us through the hotel's history, an overview of its parent company and their customer service standards, I started to feel excited again. Languishing in my dingy apartment for the past ten days had taken some of the sheen off of my Florida experience, but now Charlie was polishing it back up again.

Or maybe it was my caffeine buzz; I had been helping myself to the Learning Centre's complimentary Starbucks coffee at regular intervals all day.

At the end of day one we were presented with our newly minted Cast Member ID cards and name tags. I had never worked in a place that needed me to carry ID or punch in and out, so I found all this quite a novelty. As I studied my ID and its gentle reminder to 'Notice, Focus, Act', I realised that it was the first bit of evidence I could hold in my hand that said I was a Duck and Tuna Cast Member, and thus tangible proof that my Disney adventure had really begun.

I arrived a bit earlier on Thursday morning so I could take full advantage of the free coffee and bagels and so that I could chat to Sara about the previous day. Then, on the stroke of nine, Hank from Security appeared and proceeded to thoroughly scare the shit out of all of us.

Under the innocuous title of 'Health and Safety Training' Hank outlined for us, in intricate detail, all the horrible ills and deaths that could befall us as employees of the hospitality industry and all the ills and deaths that could befall others due to our negligence and stupidity.

'Now that you work in a hotel,' he began, 'you WILL be exposed to Hepatitis and AIDS.'

The entire room gulped like cartoon characters.

Hank wore a Nextel radio on his belt, which he and his Security cronies used as walkie-talkies; he apologised for not being able to turn it off because if an emergency were to occur he had to be reachable. Likewise, there was a television in Security that was always on and tuned to a 24-hour news station, as theme parks were high on the list of probable terrorist targets in post-9/11 America.

He had a special warning for the unfortunates among us who would get to carry a Master Key, an electronic key card that could open any one of the hotel's thousands of guest bedroom doors. Losing a Master Key was basically the worst possible thing you could do in the world after intentionally drowning a puppy; and going home with a Master Key in your pocket only slightest less disastrous. Should a Master Key go missing, it meant that every single one of the hotel's 2,265 room keys had to be reprogrammed manually as a precaution, no matter what time of the day or night.

But Hank's favourite topics seemed to be dead bodies and blood-borne diseases; every one of his nightmare hypotheticals involved one or the other.

First he targeted Sara, knowing that she would soon be working with children. If a toddler, Hank postulated, fell by the pool and cut himself, and then came running towards Sara crying with outstretched arms, what would be her gut reaction?

'I guess I'd pick the kid up,' Sara said.

'NO!' Hank roared. 'You have just picked up AN AIDS BABY! You have just contracted AIDS!'

Although I suspected a fatal flaw in his logic, his delivery was effective. The room was left wide-eyed and with an irrational fear of crying toddlers.

His next victim was a girl headed to the kitchens to work as a chef. Having warned us all that under no circumstances were we ever to approach electrical switches that bore a sign indicating they had been switched off for maintenance, he asked the girl what she should do if her direct line manager told her to turn them back on.

'I...shouldn't?' she replied, her voice almost a whisper.

'Damn *right* you shouldn't!' Hank's eyes glared deep down into the poor chef's soul. 'Because let's say you *did* flip those switches.' He paced back and forth at the top of the room. 'Let's say you obeyed your manager's orders and you turned the power back on. Then, let's say, you go out to the swimming pool, where two of our engineers have been doing some repair work – retiling, let's say.'

The air was deathly still.

'But now, because of *you*, instead of two engineers out in our swimming pool, we have two DEAD BODIES. Two DEAD BODIES, floating on top of the water. You have just, my friend, ELECTROCUTED two of our ENGINEERS! You've KILLED them.'

But that wasn't even the worst of it.

The biggest danger to ourselves and to our guests was a fire, a 'confirmed Code One.' Hank showed us how to use a fire extinguisher, directed guest evacuation instructions my way (because Front Desk would be doing it) and then spent five minutes telling us repeatedly not to do stupid things like run back in for purses, wallets or friends.

'I don't want to come back in here,' Hank said, 'after the emergency services have done their job and the fire's out, and we're all happy because' – he smiled demonically – 'we think all our guests and Cast Members are safe and well, and we think we got lucky, just so I can walk back in here and discover your CHARRED and BLACKENED BODY lying on the floor, all because you were dumb enough to run back in here for your KEYS!'

I silently vowed to myself that I would be the safest Cast Member in the history of Cast Members.

Over the course of the morning, Hank warned us against reaching into trash cans (because you might stick yourself with an AIDS needle), incorrectly labelling bottles of chemical (lest we wash our eyes out with acetone), walking fast (because we might slip, trip or crash into something), letting people we didn't know enter guest rooms with us (because they might rape or murder us), giving room keys to people claiming to be guests without checking their ID (because they might rape or murder someone else), giving our keys to other Cast Members (because they might rape or murder someone and we'd get the blame) and parking in rows one through five (because we'd get towed).

Sara and I exchanged looks. Neither of us had worked in a hotel before and no one had told us it was such a perilous job.

Being a Level 4 virologist in a poorly-funded Ebola lab was starting to sound safer.

The next morning I began somewhat more job-specific

training for my new role as a Front Desk Agent.

Ted, who had checked me in three weeks before, came to pick me up from Security. He guided us out of the maze of Backstage corridors and into the lobby, where an unmarked door led to the office hidden discreetly behind the front desk. Kelly, the Training Manager who'd decided to hire me in the first place, was running late and so while we waited for her Ted and I sat in the cramped training office and made small talk. After we had discussed Ireland, Plantation Park and the Million Dollar J-1 Question ('So, what made you decide to come here?'), Ted said, 'I heard a rumour about you.'

I scanned my recent past looking for some incident of drunken depravity, embarrassment or criminal activity that might have managed to arrive in Florida ahead of me, but found none.

To my blank expression, he said, 'I hear you'll be walking to work.'

He could have said, 'I hear you find Donald Duck arousing' in the same tone of voice. Everyone in Florida over the age of sixteen had a driver's license and people owned cars even when they couldn't afford food, clothes or shelter. I was the only one in my Orientation class who didn't need a parking permit and that included the other J-1s.

'Well, I don't have a car,' I explained.

'Oh. But you can drive, right?'

'Actually, no. I never learned. Didn't really need to.'

It was a conversation I would have another 3,205 times over the next six months.

Later Ted brought me out to the main office and made introductions. Barry, an Assistant Front Office Manager, seemed – like everyone else – genuinely helpful and friendly, talking me through something he was doing with the hotel's guest request system. Then he produced a business card and wrote his cell phone number on the back.

'I live right by the Premium Outlets,' he said,

handing it to me, 'and I pass by Plantation Park every morning on the way to work. So if we're on the same shift, just give me a call and I'll pick you up on my way in, if you want.'

Oh, brother.

I hadn't worked a day at the desk and yet I was already That Girl Who Walks to Work. News of my radical (for Orlando) transportation methods was evidently spreading through the department like the plague. The last thing I wanted was a pity party, so I assured everyone that I was absolutely fine (a lie), that I enjoyed the exercise (a joke) and that I was planning on learning to drive and buying a car in the near future (a financial impossibility).

When Kelly arrived she was as bubbly in person as she had sounded over the phone back in May. She was also tall, blonde, slim and pretty *and* she had just got engaged. If she hadn't been so nice, it would have been easy to hate her.

She asked me where I was living, how I'd got on at Orientation and if everything had been okay for me so far and unlike Casting Caroline, seemed to genuinely care if it had.

Then she said, 'Is it true you're going to *walk* to work?'

Training began with two days of classroom learning: Front Office procedures, the computer system and customer service skills, for which I was paired with fellow trainee Don who had transferred from another department within the hotel.

Despite this department having been wholly unrelated to Front Desk, his role having involved no guest contact, and having been something that happened overnight when the hotel was an entirely different place, Don seemed to think he already knew everything there was to know about being a Front Desk Agent. His delusion was so great that even with all evidence to the contrary, he still managed to maintain an air of four parts total self-assuredness, one part disinterest. With both Ted and Kelly way too nice to say anything directly, his misplaced confidence grew worse by the hour. And this was on top of his being half an hour late to his first day of training.

If the rest of the agents were anything like him, I'd be Employee of the Year in no time.

On the third day it was time to try and do the real thing on the desk.

I arrived at the hotel twenty minutes ahead of my shift and headed to the locker room, where I changed into my new 'Costume' (a brown skirt-suit flecked with what might have been green or blue or both, a synthetic blue blouse to wear underneath it and a scarf to tie artfully around one's neck), clipped my hair back securely, slipped on the dress shoes I'd bought for seven dollars at Wal-Mart and fixed my name-tag to my right lapel.

Appraising myself in the mirror, I felt the pride of a soldier in full regalia and terror at the thought that, with me dressed like this, guests would be encouraged to ask me for directions and information, neither of which I was yet equipped to give.

At the Duck desk – we were starting small, on the quieter side of the hotel – Don and I took side-by-side terminals while Ted stood between us. We wore 'In Training' badges below our name-tags, which got one of two reactions: either the guest would frown and look at their watch, intimating that they simply didn't have the time *for a trainee*, or they would exhibit saintly patience while we fumbled through their check-in and smile encouragingly.

When one of my guests went so far as to fake disbelief that this was first day on the desk, I smiled like a schoolgirl who had just had a little gold star stuck to her forehead. *I am great, aren't I?* Ted even told me that I was 'born for this gig' and although for all I knew he said that to all the girls, having reached the end of my first shift with no major errors, complaints or pissed-off guests, I was inclined to agree with him. I skipped all the way back to Plantation Park, thinking that all of that dropping out of college business had happened for a reason; I was *supposed* to do this.

But then on my second desk day, all hell broke loose.

Once a year, a huge tech symposium descends on Walt Disney World. With guest rooms filled with people busy during the day, it's a great time to visit the parks but it's a bad time to be a Front Desk Agent, and it's a horrific time to be in training as one.

Don and I were scheduled to be on the Tuna side, where – get this – over *one thousand guests* were expected to check-in in a single day. Despite every available agent manning a terminal, there was still a long line snaking through the lobby and threatening to head outside.

I was terrified, and appropriately so; still only in training, I wasn't ready to deal with anything other than a simple, straightforward check-in and those were thin on the ground today. I took a deep breath, braced myself, and headed into the fray.

Not five minutes passed before I was met with my first disaster. One of our suites had been reserved for the financial director of a well-known computer company. Due to my fleeting teenage obsession with all things Silicon Valley, I recognised the man's name as soon as it appeared on my screen. I was fairly certain, however, that even though I had never seen his picture, the fresh-faced twenty-odd year old in front of me wasn't him.

'I'm with his security detail,' the young guy explained, lowering his voice so the guests on either side of him couldn't hear; it was all very Secret Service. 'We need to sweep the room before he arrives.'

At that precise moment, everyone around me and in

the back office was already up to their eyeballs with other issues and, two terminals along, Ted and Don were stuck with another guest, and so I was on my own. Fresh-Faced Guy's name was nowhere on the reservation and, by God, I wasn't about to ignore any of Hank's dire warnings, so I politely explained that I couldn't provide him with a key. I presumed that if anything, he would appreciate my caution and my efforts to keep his client safe.

I presumed wrong.

He 'went postal' as my American colleagues liked to say, and demanded that I get a manager. When she came out, he gave her an earful about my incompetence – while I stood there beside her – and stalked off in a huff, but with a key. Earlier in the day he and his team had made arrangements with Front Desk to collect a key ahead of time, but this information hadn't found its way to me, a lowly trainee, and if it had, I probably wouldn't have known what to do with it.

Next in line at my terminal was a guest whose company had booked him in under the wrong name. Unfortunately this error didn't come to light for nearly ten minutes, the same ten minutes I spent telling him that he didn't have a room and that the hotel was booked out. A trembling vein on my guest's forehead looked close to bursting when I realised that Ted was free and motioned for him to come help me. Needless to say, he quickly found the reservation and the guest stormed off to his room, no doubt thinking that I was the most stupid person who had ever lived, which was what I was beginning to think too.

After a terrifying hour or two, Ted announced that we could head back to the tranquil environs of the Duck side, words I was unnaturally relieved to hear. But as we went to walk out through the back office, one of the Rooms Control Supervisors swung round in his chair and started screaming at Ted.

'They're not saving their check-ins!' he roared,

meaning Don and I. 'I've just had three people in a row get keys for rooms that were already occupied. You're the one who's supposed to be watching them, you should have noticed.'

I wanted to crawl under the photocopier and cry. This was the first time in my working life I had ever been shouted at – even secondhand - and it didn't feel nice. I understood that everyone was under pressure and having just as bad or a worse day than us, but combined with the chaos we had just left on the other side of the wall, it was all too much to take.

A year later, I'd still be having nightmares about The Day of a Thousand Check-Ins, regaling new trainees with the story of how my first day on the Tuna desk had also been the busiest day of the year. They were invariably impressed, or at least pretended to be. Luckily I was to be permanently stationed at the Duck wing of the hotel, the quieter side.

The following day, Kelly and Ted marked the end of our training with a treasure hunt/learning exercise that involved a very uncomfortable Friendship ride to Epcot's International Gateway entrance during which Don kept invading my personal space, and the awarding of welcome presents. Kelly had bought us each a stapler and a 'Payday' chocolate bar, thrown in a stress ball emblazoned with the corporate logo and an inspirational quote, wrapped the whole thing in cellophane and tied it with ribbons. It was a really nice touch.

Then it was off onto the desk, alone.

I kept hold of my 'In Training' badge, just in case.

Despite the shaky start, by the end of my first week as a Front Desk Agent I knew I was going to love my job. I'd also met many of the Cast of Characters who would play both major and minor roles in my Orlando life.

My most frequent partner on the desk was Miho, a demure Japanese woman who'd studied hospitality in the US and whose visa, unfortunately, was set to expire after Christmas. She constantly strived to be polite and precise, and to improve upon her heavily accented English which was already very good. She kept a small notebook on her at all times in which she jotted down updated Disney information and new English phrases she'd picked up during the day. One of the sentences she copied down in her tiny, precise handwriting was the one I used to direct guests to our West Elevators: 'Take a left at the corner and go all the way down to the end.'

If we were joined by a third agent it was usually Mark, a tall, tanned and beautiful Floridian who was a big hit with the guests, and whom I bonded with over a shared love of office gossip and the TV show 24. Mark also delighted in sharing the intimate details of his gay sex life with me over lunch, no matter how much I protested.

Then there were the Three Amigos: Will, Neil and Shawn. Will and Neil both worked in the back office, while Shawn had the same job as me but at the Tuna. If two of them weren't concocting a practical joke to play on the third then they were planning a payday drinking session or making up a new nickname for one of the rest of us. Mine, predictably, was Lucky Charms, thanks to the popular breakfast cereal hawked by a deranged, sugar-crazed leprechaun whose catch phrase is, 'They're after me Lucky Charms!'

Sometimes we worked with Oscar, a serious and quiet addition to our team who was a little bit older and thus had some maturity on the Three Amigos, Mark and myself. He was the first to answer a question or explain a procedure, and was a great help to a clueless newbie like me.

But while the bonds of friendship formed at work, outside of it I was alone, and this was completely my own doing. Every Wednesday night there was a large gathering of Front Desk people at a bar on International Drive, and each week someone would think to invite me, but I always declined. I *had* to. How could I even begin to explain the trouble I'd have to go to just to join them for a drink?

I'd arrived in Florida with my head in a cloud of pixie dust, ill-prepared for the costs of setting up a life there. My financial situation only got worse when an entire month passed by without a paycheck. I couldn't afford to spend money on a cab ride to the grocery store, much less one to I-Drive and back just so I could have a drink with my colleagues. And I would rather have streaked naked through the lobby at check-out time than ask someone I'd known for less than a month to drive to my apartment to pick me up and then drive me home again later, even though these were nice people and they would tell me later that they would have been happy to do so.

Every day I stood behind the desk, all smiles. I greeted guests with genuine enthusiasm and shared a laugh with my colleagues. Anyone would have assumed I was enjoying my new life and was happy to have made the decision to move here. But by the end of October I'd been in Orlando for two months and had yet to find any elements of my imagined Florida life in its real world equivalent.

And that had me worried.

Six
STOP THIS TRAIN

When November arrived, I barely recognised it. The sun still shone every day and the temperature and humidity only let up by one degree.

Sunlight seems different in Central Florida. In his novel *All Families Are Psychotic*, Douglas Coupland calls it a 'prehistoric glare', a harsh sun mercilessly reflected off the plastic horror down below, as strong and unbroken as it must have been back when dinosaurs roamed the earth beneath a thin, sparse atmosphere. There is no haze, no cloud, no respite, and I had to walk to work in it every day.

I wasn't exactly loving the walking to work, but I was getting used to it. (It was also helping me achieve the skinnier version of me I'd seen running around Magic Kingdom in my mind's eye.) My daily routine went something like this: fall out of bed at noon, have a cup of instant coffee for breakfast, walk for forty minutes through intense heat and blinding sun to the bus stop at Downtown Disney's Marketplace, use the twenty minute air-conditioned bus journey as an opportunity to cool down before I got to the hotel where I'd arrive fifteen minutes before my shift and with just enough time to change in my costume and grab a cold Coke. Sometimes the bus would be a few minutes late; on those days, Will always remarked on the flushed cheeks I showed up with at our pre-shift meeting.

Meanwhile my life was running entirely within the confines of the small triangle formed by my crappy apartment, Downtown Disney and the hotel, and not by choice. I was trapped inside it. My cell phone was Virgin Mobile because the only place within walking distance that sold phones was Westside's Virgin Megastore. My bank account was with Sun Trust because they had a branch on Hotel Plaza Boulevard, the street that stretched between my local Disney gates and my Disney bus stop. If I was at home and hungry, I ordered in. When I needed some new T-shirts, I bought them at online at The Gap. If I needed coffee, milk or sugar, I'd sneak over to the Tuna wing of the hotel after work and buy it in their 24-hour-convenience store at twice the regular price. To get home from work, I'd change back into my own clothes and walk around the back of the hotel to the adjacent Boardwalk Inn, because I didn't want any of our bellmen or valets to see me having to take a cab home.

But the nights were the real problem. Getting home around midnight, I'd lie in my scratchy Wal-Mart sheets and wonder why the Orlando I now lived in – a highway of strip malls, a Disney shopping mall, work – was so different to the Orlando I'd been promised.

During the day it was exhausting keeping up a pretence of happiness while I waited for things to get better – or at least easier – and so by the end of every day, I just couldn't muster the effort required to keep up that same pretence with myself. Even the smallest thing – getting to work, buying a carton of milk, cashing a pay check – took so much effort. I felt like I could never relax, that I was under constant pressure. I worried that soon, some little slip – an angry guest or a missed bus, for instance – would destroy my outward equilibrium, the taunt surface tension would be broken and the darkness would be out as well as in, on show, right there for everyone to see.

What I wasn't paying much attention to at the time was that I was also suffering from a far more serious problem than self-pitying Central Floridian angst, and that was an inability to sleep. I'd toss and turn into the dawn hours, absolutely spent but unable to close my eyes for more than a few minutes. Each day I nudged closer and closer to complete and utter exhaustion, which seemed to magnify my Orlando-related worries, which made it more difficult to sleep, and so on and so on in a vicious, never-ending cycle.

But it wasn't until an incident aboard a Disney shuttle bus in early November that I realised just how much of a certifiable nutcase this combination of lack of sleep and unease had turned me into. If something didn't change, it would no doubt be only a few more years before I'd be hoarding plastic bags in a house full of cats, muttering to myself as I wandered around in a dirty housecoat.

This time, it was all John Mayer's fault.

I had treated myself to his new album, *Continuum*, which arrived in the mail just in time for me to upload it to my iPod and run out the door to work. Which is how, around an hour later, I came to be standing on a crowded Disney bus, hearing the song 'Stop This Train' for the first ever time. And let me just stress for the record how crowded this bus was - I was standing in the aisle, holding onto a rail above my head while the face of the person next me got to know my armpit.

The song started out innocuously enough. But when the lyrics kicked in, featuring repetition of the phrase, 'Stop this train, I want to get off and go home again', they were acidic, instantly dissolving the tenuous bond that up until then had just about been holding me together.

For slightly depressed, totally exhausted and potentially emotionally unstable me, standing on a

Disney bus thousands of miles from home and possibly regretting the decisions that had brought me here, musical accompaniment didn't come much more devastating than this, except for maybe that cheery number 'Everybody Hurts' by REM.

I came undone; I broke open, I broke apart. I was suddenly standing there, in the middle of a crowded bus of sunburned vacationers, holding back tears so heavy they threatened to skip my cheeks and head straight for the floor.

A cursory glance at my life might lead you to believe that I had arrived in Florida recklessly unprepared and thus found myself in an unfavourable situation designed by my own hand. But nothing was ever that black and white with me. Lurking underneath was a murky greyness with roots, repercussions, chains of events. Or, in other words, self-psychoanalysis, using an amalgamation of techniques gleaned from *Oprah*, Barnes and Noble's self-help section and a whole adolescence's worth of talking too much about everything.

Applying these methods to myself as I lay awake at night had led me to the following conclusion:

I had come to Florida for the same reason I'd done everything else, because I was searching for happiness, a place where I felt happy. Nice home, nice view, nice friends, nice job, nice guy. The only place I knew for sure these things didn't exist was back home in Ireland which left...well, pretty much the rest of the world to sift through. (Except for Australia. Due to a steady influx of Irish twenty-somethings, Sydney was basically Ireland with sunny weather, which I considered to be only a marginal improvement.) But despite many happy times and memories to match them, Holland had had to come to an end and now, the Florida of my mind's eye was seemingly grossly off-target, pushing me to move on again.

But this time I wasn't just here for a short season with no lasting effects, but eighteen months – long enough to be the real thing. And it seemed too hard, it was taking too much effort. And the worst thought of all, the one that kept me up night after night, alone in my apartment and starved of sleep and perspective, was the thought that *this was it*. This was what my life would always be like, moving from place to place, starting from scratch over and over, always looking, never finding.

The ugly truth was that if I decided to jack this all in and go home, there was nowhere else to go but another Orlando. Pack up everything, move somewhere else, start again. I couldn't go back to Ireland because more than seven consecutive nights there and I'd break out in hives. I had no choice but to hold on, but I was so exhausted.

I was also actively engineering my own loneliness. I had pushed myself towards unyielding independence, the Ice Queen who didn't need anyone but herself. (And her parents, when the money ran low.) But where had it got me? Thousands of miles away from my family and friends, splayed on a thin mattress in a room as sparse as a prison cell, crying myself to sleep as the sun rose in the sky.

I had made this much bigger than having to walk to the grocery store. I was mourning all the things I'd ever had reason to be sad about, all those half-hearted assertions, promises, decisions, the dreams I'd (somewhat prematurely) announced to the world; I was a disappointment to everybody, they pitied me, they thought it was all such a shame, they thought I was wasting my life. I was languishing in that little room in Orlando, acutely aware that my twenties – the one decade when you're both old enough and young enough to do whatever it is you want and get away with it – were steaming at full speed to the mid-way point, not unlike...*hey, just like a train!*

On the Disney bus, the other passengers had turned to stare at me.

Seven
INTO THE KINGDOM

If things had continued down that path, who knows where I'd be today? (Although wherever it is, I bet there are lots of cats.) But instead, I met Eva.

Eva was a German J-1 who worked at the Tuna wing of the hotel, but who, several weeks into my program, I still hadn't met. Amazingly, we were not only colleagues but neighbours as well; Eva lived on the other side of Plantation Park. When we finally did meet one day on the Tuna desk, we were instant friends.

We shared with each other our grievances against the United States (bad TV, terrible geographical knowledge, the word 'awesome') and what we perceived to be our innate superiority as forward-thinking Europeans. We both had a similar sense of humour and liked to do things our Floridian friends found unacceptably touristy, such as sightseeing.

Eva had already spent a year working at Epcot's Germany pavilion and had returned to Orlando fully prepared with an apartment, a roommate and a car lined up. Having only arrived four weeks before me, she appeared to already have a fully formed life here, complete with a circle of friends and a suntan, and she seemed to *love* Orlando.

She was pretty much living exactly the kind of life I'd imagined I would be before I got here. But that was okay, because she was about to bring me along for the ride.

Within minutes of meeting her, she offered to drive me to and from work. Since we lived in the same complex and worked many of the same shifts, I could hardly refuse the offer on the grounds that I'd be an unnecessary burden, like I usually did. So now, instead of leaving my apartment two hours ahead of time and suffering through the heat, I'd meet Eva at two-thirty and we'd drive in together. On the journey back at the end of the night we'd swap any office gossip we'd acquired during the day and if there was too much of it to cover in the ten-minute journey, I'd call over to her place afterwards to complete its telling. (Her apartment was much nicer than mine, since it had furniture and decorations and stuff, i.e. it looked like somebody actually *lived* there.)

Through Eva, I began to see the Orlando that lay beyond my triangulated prison. We'd go to Dr Philips, an upscale neighbourhood nearby, and browse the shelves of Barnes and Noble (my idea of heaven), before having a turkey and brie sandwich (Eva) and a tomato and mozzarella salad (me) at Press 101. We'd stroll around the Florida Mall, or grocery shop after work at the Wal-Mart Super Centre on 535. We also had many a movie night as I tried to expose Eva to all the films whose release she'd appeared to have missed (clue: all of them) and, on the occasional Friday, we hit our local Buffalo Wild Wings for Ladies Night and no, it wasn't any classier than it sounds. Because I was spending more time with Eva, I was spending more time with the rest of the Front Desk crew by extension and on Wednesday nights you might even find me having a payday drink at a bar on I-Drive.

It wasn't as if I was suddenly high on pixie dust, but my Orlando life had changed dramatically. By mid-

November, I was actually having one.

I knew this for sure when, just after Thanksgiving, Eva brought me into the parks.

Her friends Clara and Toby were visiting from Philadelphia where they'd been working for Siemens. Eva planned to bring them into Epcot and Magic Kingdom and when she discovered I was off work the same day, she invited me along. Two and half months after arriving in Florida (and after eight weeks of winging it with guests looking for park information), I was finally going to see what all the fuss was about.

We left Eva's apartment shortly after eight that morning. As per usual, the sky was clear and the sun was shining brightly, but it was surprisingly cold. Not just Florida cold (when you can roll down the windows of your car without suffocating) but *actual* cold (when you turn on the heat instead). Clara and Toby wore jackets while Eva and I, the brave Floridians, put sweaters over our T-shirts. Since Eva and I were Cast Members in name only – the Duck and Tuna wasn't owned by Disney – we had to pay to enter the parks. Luckily, a former manager of Eva's kindly met us at the Epcot turnstiles and signed us all in as his guests, granting each of us access to all of the Disney parks for the rest of the day for free.

Epcot is divided into two main areas, Future World and the World Showcase. The main entrance leads you underneath the Monorail tracks and brings you into Future World, right at the base of the park's iconic structure, the 180 foot white geodesic sphere - more commonly known as the giant golf ball - that houses the Spaceship Earth attraction. Beyond it, we caught glimpses of the rest of the park: imposing, angular structures with smooth, reflective facades, spinning accents of gleaming fan blades and powerful fountains shooting columns of white water high into the air.

Disney's version of the future was already defunct

before the Imagineers had even finished drawing the plans; it was what space-age looked like before we went there. Although this clean and shiny future had failed to transpire, it did have a comforting innocence to it, and an admirable hope.

We decided to start our day by riding Spaceship Earth, billed as a tour through mankind's advances in communication. Almost everything in Future World has a corporate sponsor, and Eva's visitors laughed when they saw that this ride was bankrolled by none other than their own employer, Siemens. After being loaded onto a small train, we were carried up and around the interior of the sphere at the breakneck speed of about four miles an hour. Audio-enhanced animatronic displays chronicled man's every effort to reach out to his neighbour, from finger painting to the World Wide Web, until a tangle of brightly coloured fibre-optic cables led us out beneath an expansive starry sky, presumably on the sphere's ceiling. Actor (and Cork resident) Jeremy Irons narrated the journey.

But throughout the entire experience I was distracted by the architecture of the sphere. How did they fit all this in here, when surely a lot of space was unusable due to the curvature? I wanted to see some schematics.

Afterwards we crossed Future World's main plaza, passing signs pointing to Wonders of Life, Universe of Energy and Innovations. Working Front Desk I had encountered many a guest complaining that Epcot was no fun for small children and now I was beginning to see why.

Eva wanted us all to ride Soarin' which she had described to me as 'a flight over California.' I was dubious about anything that might lift me, drop me, throw me or spin me, but Eva claimed that not only was this ride mild, but that it was probably the best one in the park. Unfortunately everyone else seemed to think so too; the Wait Time was already an hour. So instead we each collected a 'FASTPASS'; a sort of VIP ticket that would enable us to come back later in the day and skip to the head of the line.

Our next stop was The Seas Pavilion, where we were anxious to experience the new *Finding Nemo* ride that had only opened a couple of weeks before. After we were ushered into our 'clam-mobiles' (giant vertical clam shells fitted with seats), we entered Nemo's underwater playground where we learned that, yet again, the little fish had run off and gone missing. Our clam-mobiles moved around the tanks of The Seas' aquarium, the Plexiglass views spruced up with some stunning coral, its colour and detail some of the Imagineers' best efforts. We passed beneath a plethora of pink jellyfish suspended from the ceiling, slowly slinking up and down, and through a long tunnel with animated walls that made us feel as if we were really riding an ocean current with our surfing turtle friend Crush and his adorable son Squirt. The finale was a sickly sweet musical number, but with a cheeky twist: the pleas of a starfish begging for you to take her with you because she just can't listen to the rest of them sing that song even one more time.

Then after an all-important mid-morning coffee, it was time to head back to Soarin' with our fantastical FASTPASSes and skip the queue.

FASTPASS 101: You arrive at an attraction only to find that you're going to be waiting an hour or more to ride it. But all is not lost because it's part of the FASTPASS system. So, you go to the special machines by the entrance, stick in your Disney admission ticket and out pops a FASTPASS. It gives you an hour-long window during which you can return, e.g. between 1pm and 2pm, and, in the meantime, you can go off and enjoy the rest of the park. Within the specified time you return to the attraction, join the FASTPASS line and, usually, get on the ride within ten to fifteen minutes. Although I'd been schooling my guests on this system for weeks, today would be the first day I'd actually use it.

The only downside to it, as I saw it, was FASTPASS

User's Guilt. So okay, it's not your fault that you're a work-smarter-not-harder type of person, or that you had the sense to, first of all, find out what the hell a FASTPASS was and, second of all, use it, but the people in the Stand By line (yes, they call the other line 'Stand By') don't know this and glare at you accusingly as if you're one of those undoers of modern civilisation, the queue-jumper. When we walked onto Soarin' that day, the people at the top of the regular line had already been waiting for almost two hours and were none too pleased to see us walk on by. The moral of this story: get yourself a FASTPASS and smile apologetically.

Having left the Stand Byers behind, we were filtered into rows just outside Soarin's theatre by a Cast Member dressed as a flight attendant, and then a burly pilot with a voice as thick as cream appeared on the TV screens in front of us to take us through a 'safety briefing.' Presently the doors opened and we took our places in the first row of seats, which hung from a large mechanism that took up the whole room and faced a large, curved screen.

A disembodied voice asked us to put all our belongings in the little basket beneath our seats and to slip out of any loose footwear - such as flip-flops - and leave them on the floor in front of us. I noticed our seats were fitted with seatbelts and handles. I was about to ask Eva what that was all about when the lights went out. We were lifted up, tilted forward, and swung closer to the screen in one swoop.

The same swoop that appeared to have us forty feet above the floor, legs dangling.

What the-

Then, courtesy of the scenes on screen and the movements of our seats, we were flying through the clouds and over the varied state of California. Wonderful touches, such as a real breeze through our hair as we passed over Malibu's coastline, or the scent of oranges as we skimmed the trees of a Camarillo grove, made it all the more magical. We were treated to a bird's eye view of the Golden Gate Bridge, San Diego's harbour and the lights of Los Angeles as they twinkled against the night sky. Our five-minute flight ended, appropriately, over Disneyland in Anaheim, where we arrived just in time for the closing fireworks. I loved every second of it.

We spent the afternoon touring the World Showcase, stopping at Germany to see the store where Eva had worked for a year, the UK to pick up some Cadbury's chocolate and Twinings tea-bags, and Canada to watch their tourist board-inspired cinematic extravaganza, *O Canada*. (It really did make me want to go there.)

Then, as the light started to fade, we hopped on the Monorail and headed for what promised to be the happiest place on earth, Magic Kingdom.

By the time we got there, the sun had gone and we were freezing. Again, not just Florida freezing but actually so; my cheeks were bright pink with the cold and my fingers felt icy.

But I wasn't complaining. I was finally in Magic Kingdom, for Mickey's sake.

We made a beeline for Fantasyland, located behind Cinderella's magnificent fairy-tale castle. Mickey's Philharmagic was one of Eva's favourite MK attractions and that day it also became one of mine. This was another theatre presentation but in 3-D; we picked up our attractive yellow plastic glasses from a bin in the holding area. When we got inside, I noticed that the seats were upholstered in wipe-clean plastic.

'They need to be waterproof,' Eva said casually.

'*Why*?' I said, spinning around.

Maestro Mickey appeared on screen, scuttling about preparing to lead his orchestra of enchanted instruments in a symphony. But when he's mysteriously distracted from the task at hand, his pal Donald Duck steps up to the plate and disaster ensues. But it's a wonderful disaster that makes its way through a host of classic

Disney musical numbers from *Aladdin, Beauty and the Beast, The Little Mermaid* and *The Lion King,* among others. Thanks to your 3-D glasses, all of it seems to be happening right in front of your face and, as with Soarin', Disney had added elements to enhance your experience. In a scene from *Fantasia,* Donald is haplessly swept away by an enchanted wet mop that splashes you as well; when dinner is served during *Be Our Guest* you can really smell the steaming apple pie; a bottle of champagne pops open and you feel the cork whizzing past your head.

It really *is* magical.

Opposite the Philharmagic theatre is the only tangible evidence I've ever gathered of Disney's rumoured evil. It's a Small World is a trippy boat ride through international hell made famous by its creepy dolls and theme song which *The Unofficial Guide to Walt Disney World* warns 'only a backhoe' can remove from your brain. We and our fellow victims were loaded onto a small boat, bid farewell by a Cast Member wearing the face of a condemned man and then taken on a leisurely cruise around the world, if the world was inhabited by third cousins of Chucky from *Child's Play,* all of whom wear traditional dress and follow your every move with their soulless black eyes of toy darkness. By the tenth repetition of the song – which seemed to have only the one line, 'it's a small world after all' – the water beneath our boat was starting to look very, very attractive.

After night had fallen we met up with Ted and Barry from work, who happened to be in the park that evening. We warmed our hands on cups of hot chocolate while we waited for them on Main Street USA (already decorated for the upcoming holidays, a fact I was actively trying to ignore) and when they arrived, we eyed their thick, warm jackets with envy. Looking for an escape from the worsening cold, we sought shelter in Pirates of the Caribbean – another boat ride, but this one was through a dark and threatening pirate lair.

A boat ride that was certainly not for feminists.

The women of Pirates all looked disconcertingly like wenches or whores; one scene had four or five of them tied together and to a man who appeared to be selling them as brides. Following the runaway success of the film franchise, a few animatronic Captain Jack Sparrows had been added to update the ride and their likeness to Johnny Depp was so amazing that I was tempted to bring one of them home with me. But by far the best thing about our Pirates experience that evening was our WDW Celebrity Sighting: Steven Tyler from Aerosmith, just ahead of us in the queue. We all tried hard not to stare at him. We all failed.

Finally and led by Barry, our little group made its way to the plaza in front of Cinderella's Castle and took up a spot just to the left of the 'Partners' statue of Walt and Mickey Mouse. We were here to watch Wishes, the fireworks show that closes the park each evening and which Disney considers to be its goodnight kiss to its guests.

The awaiting crowd seemed keyed up and excited, their anticipation palpable, but I had no clue what to expect.

As soon as the clock struck ten, lights dimmed all over the park and music began playing quietly, building to a loud crescendo as a lone star and its sparkling trail jumped over the castle. A female voice began, 'When stars are born, they possess a dream or two. One of them is this: they have the power to make a wish come true!'

When I heard these words - talk of dreams and wishes - followed by something that sounded like 'When You Wish Upon a Star', I knew I was in trouble.

For the next twenty-five minutes, the most magnificent fireworks display I have ever seen threw itself into the sky above me. While Jiminy Cricket narrated with the occasional help of the Blue Fairy, each burst of light was timed to coincide exactly with a movement in the music, as Disney characters such as *Aladdin's* Genie shared their wishes and dreams with us.

On at least two occasions the crowd applauded, thinking they had just seen the finale, only to have the display continue on a moment later, bigger and better.

They – and I – hadn't seen anything yet.

While I watched, everything else went away. I was no longer lonely, disappointed, or anything of the other things my sleep deprivation-induced loss of perspective had convinced me I was. Instead, I felt filled with as much light as the sky.

For two and a half months I'd been stuck in one tiny corner of Orlando and my view of Walt Disney World had been that of an outsider: shuttle buses, merchandise stores and the Boardwalk. Today was my first beyond the turnstiles. And so how could I have known that this wonderful world was here too?

Here in Magic Kingdom, happiness and magic were practically on tap and, even if they were manufactured, my response to them was real. Watching Wishes was better than anything a good night's sleep, a full photo album of smiling faces or even a prescription for Prozac could do for me. I looked around at our little group; here were Eva, Ted, Barry and I standing in Magic Kingdom, faces turned towards the sky, watching fireworks.

Yeah, just your typical Tuesday night in Orlando.

As every inch of the sky beyond the castle's turrets blazed with the show's climax and the accompanying song encouraged us to trust our hearts so our wishes could come true, the crowd burst into spontaneous applause. I felt giddy and light-headed. It was like Magic Kingdom had known exactly what I needed: a reminder of how much I believed in dreams, and a push to start believing in this one.

In this land of make-believe, I'd found what I'd been looking for. It was right there in front of me, all over the sky. This was why I'd come to Orlando; this was why I'd wanted to work in Disney World.

That night, I slept like a baby.

Eight
SORT OF HAPPY HOLIDAYS

So the good news was that my Orlando life was changing for the better.

The bad news was that you can only sniff so much pixie dust in one day at Disney and I would need a whole lot more of it to get through what was coming ever closer: my first Christmas away from home. Unless Tinkerbell started moonlighting as a dust dealer, I was about to spend the month of December choking on my own childish tears.

The problem was that I was one of those rare hybrid breeds: an Irish, Christmas-crazed atheist. Although Christmas holds absolutely no religious significance for me - apart from the fact that it's the one day of the year my father can be relied upon to say, 'Wouldn't you ever go to Mass today, Catherine? I mean, for God's sake, it's *Christmas!*' - I completely adore the holiday season that has sprung up around it, even if the only non-earthling I associate with December 25th wears red, advertises Coke and rides a sleigh.

I love Christmas trees, fairy lights, fancy giftwrap and a valid excuse to overeat. I love Christmas present shopping even if it means I have to fight my way through frenzied crowds. I love carol singers, TV specials and movies set in New York at Christmastime, like *Serendipity* and *Home Alone* 2. I love decorating the whole house in green, red and gold and then taking photos of it to send to *Ideal Homes* magazine (because, I'll have you know, Christmas decorating happens to be one of my many gifts, if I do say so myself). I love writing Christmas cards and mailing them with special Christmas-themed stamps. In short, I love everything about it.

Just not the Jesus stuff.

But in all my twenty-four years, I had never been away from home for it. This would be the first time and I was *dreading* it.

Late one Friday night at the beginning of December, I returned home from work to find a note stuck in the door that read, 'Locks changed. New key in clubhouse. After 11pm, call me. James.'

Eva had just dropped me off and I was supposed to be back at her apartment, changed and ready for Ladies' Night, as soon as humanly possible. The clubhouse staff had long gone home, so I was left with no choice but to call James. It took him nearly half an hour to arrive with the new key, which I snatched out of his hand without a word, stormed furiously into the apartment, and slammed the door shut behind me.

The next day, I got new roommates.

They were three women from the Philippines, ranging in age from twenty to thirty-five, who had just got jobs as housekeepers in the Marriot across the street from Plantation Park. After the Kazaks they were a joy. Far from throwing wild parties or making noise at crazy o'clock, they called me 'Miss Catherine', cleaned the kitchen until it began to disintegrate and tip-toed around the living room in the mornings, no matter how many times I insisted that I could easily sleep through their breakfast making and chit-chat. With them working nine to five and me working three to eleven, we fell easily into a routine that was workable for everyone. When they got home, I'd still be at work and I wouldn't get back until after they went to bed. They got to watch their bible-thumping Christian programming and I got to watch my nightly menu of Leno, *The Daily Show* and *The Colbert Report*.

Meanwhile, Christmas was everywhere. It's not allowed to sneak up on you in Disney World, it just appears. One day there isn't a trace of it and then the next it looks like Santa's been sick all over the parks during the night.

Once Halloween is done with and under the cover of darkness, all the Disney elves come out of the Mickey Mouse-Shaped Things Factory and decorate every square inch of the property with lights, trees and poinsettias. By the time dawn breaks, the entire place is well and truly festified. Tack on some additional 'holiday' fireworks to the end of Wishes and Illumi-NATIONS, install Santa on Main Street USA, switch out all the piped muzak CDs for carol compilations and the metamorphosis is complete: you're all set for a Disney Christmas.

At the desk I gritted my teeth as professional decorators arrived to cover the place in garlands and erect an enormous tree made of white, pink and green leaves interwoven with fairy lights in the Tuna's Rotunda Lobby. It was circled by an oversized toy train and topped, somewhat inexplicably, with a gigantic mirror ball. Back at the Duck, I moved to a terminal behind one of the lobby's support columns so I wouldn't have to stare at our Christmas tree all day while I worked.

The temperature dropped but not by much, and Central Floridians stayed in their unofficial uniform of jeans, a T-shirt and flip-flops. There was already something terribly wrong with the juxtaposition of poinsettias and palm trees but now, on top of that, a hot humid Christmas looked to be on the cards as well.

If anything, I thought this would help.

If it didn't *feel* like Christmas then I might be able to pretend it wasn't.

But I did want to experience Disney World at Christmas, something I might never have the chance to do again (I'd already made up my mind that next Christmas, I was going to fly home for a fortnight) and so I decided to go with Miho to Mickey's Very Merry Christmas Party.

This was a special ticketed event held at Magic Kingdom on selected evenings throughout the holiday season. It promised festive shows and parades, snow falling on Main Street, Santa Claus himself and free/included in the ticket price hot cocoa and cookies for all guests. I could barely contain myself at the thought of the party's finale: a specially extended holiday version of Wishes.

Miho and I arrived at the gates of Magic Kingdom with just one objective in mind: to see and experience absolutely everything on the MVMCP programme (two special Christmas shows, a SpectroMagic parade, Wishes and the chance to meet Santa Claus next to Main Street's Town Hall), as well as however many regular rides and attractions we could fit in. The beauty of the programme was that most things were on twice, giving Miho and I two choices to catch all the shows and plenty of opportunities to run onto rides in between.

We executed our plan with near-military precision, picking up our cocoa and cookies as we ran about the park. We started by grabbing some dinner (read: fuel) at Tomorrowland's Starlight Cafe, cleverly avoiding the dinnertime rush. This left us with ample time to secure a good viewing spot in front of Cinderella's Castle for Celebrate the Season, a special festive show featuring Mickey, Minnie, the Disney Princesses and all their charming man-friends. After touring our favourite mouse couple's country homes in Mickey's Toontown Fair, we met the big – or little – mouse himself in the adjacent Judge's Tent.

As we stood in line for a photo with him, I wondered how he had got here so quickly from his show at the Castle...

On our way back to Fantasyland, we spotted Donald Duck in his seasonal role as a Christmas tree salesman (or salesduck?) outside Ariel's Grotto, so we lined up for a quick picture. The characters are elusive creatures and you need to seize your photo ops whenever you can.

Afterwards we hit The Many Adventures of Winnie the Pooh, Peter Pan's Flight and Philharmagic, all within the space of forty minutes because the Wait Times for each were negligible. We followed this up with a run back past Toontown and into Tomorrowland's Galaxy Theatre, where we were treated to Disney's all-singing, all-dancing, all-green-and-red-wearing version of *'Twas the Night Before Christmas*. Afterwards we worked our way from Thunder Mountain to Pirates to the Jungle Cruise, which looked closed until a lone Cast Member emerged from the dark and ushered us onto a boat.

Unfortunately, other than our Cast Member Captain, we were the only two people on it.

The Jungle Cruise, as the name suggests, is a cruise through the jungle. During the day, Disney's meandering Amazonian waterway dotted with animatronic crocs, bathing elephants and hissing snakes seems outdated and a bit, well – as the kids say – *crap*. Nightfall does help, prohibiting guests from seeing anything other than the murky green water immediately beyond the boat, creeping foliage and whatever the narrow beam of the bow's searchlight happens to hit.

But that's just the scenery. The real pull of the Jungle Cruise is the team of amateur comedians that Disney hires to steer the boats, best known for their flagrant use of clichés and snide remarks. I once had a Jungle Cruise Captain, for example, who told us how proud her parents were that after four years of university and thousands of pounds on visa fees, she had landed a job as a Disney ride operator, paid by the hour and with no benefits. Another bade good-bye to the elephants with the words, 'I'll see you guys again,' before adding wryly, 'in about fifteen minutes.' But tonight the comedy routine fell flat on our near empty boat, although not from lack of effort.

Pleased with our selves and our perfectly executed plan, I brought Miho to the same spot Barry had brought me only a couple of weeks earlier to watch Wishes. Tonight, Cinderella's Castle was stunning, lit with blue light while snowflakes danced on its walls. Wishes seemed to be even bigger and brighter than I remembered – which was saying something – but this time it made me think not of myself but of my family, and how they weren't here.

Everything I was seeing was another thing they were not. I could imagine them here beside me: Dad mildly entertained but not impressed, Mum snapping pictures that would never get developed, John taking it all in while Claire, the adolescent of the family, rolled her eyes and pretended she didn't know us. I'd sent them photographs and video clips, but they couldn't convey what it was like to stand in the arms of Disney's magic in the those days before Christmas, sipping hot chocolate beneath an enchanted sky, walking back down Main Street USA as the evening drew to a close with (fake foam) snow falling on your shoulders, happy, smiling faces everywhere.

And 'I'll Be Home for Christmas' playing on repeat.

If I have to listen to that bloody song one more time, I swear...

It was nearly midnight by the time we reached Main Street's Town Hall and the line of people waiting to take a seat on Santa's knee. Meeting the Big Man Himself was the only thing on the MVMCP program we'd thus far failed to do, so we joined the queue. A moment later a Cast Member appeared to inform everyone in line behind us that Santa was done for the day; we'd just made it.

Nearly another hour passed before Santa got round to us. Our faces blanched as he offered us each a knee, but then this was Disney, not the mall. Disappointingly he didn't ask us what we wanted for Christmas, but I would have been straight in there with, 'John Mayer –

and I don't mean on CD', if he had.

After the festive fun of Mickey's Very Merry Christmas Party my stockpile of holiday spirit was quickly depleted, so much so that I wasn't going to have enough to get through the night of the Cast Christmas Party intact.

Being a newbie, I was scheduled to work through the entire thing so those who had been newbies last year could attend the party. At first I was actually happy with this arrangement because it meant I could avoid it altogether, but as the night grew closer and Eva – who had requested the night off as this would be her only Cast Christmas Party – started to get excited about it, it started to suck big time, not to get too poetic.

Mark and I were the agents that evening, working while we watched our colleagues and friends arrive for the party. Our manager encouraged us to take our lunch breaks over there, but I would have been mortified to walk into a ballroom of evening dresses in my dowdy Costume, no matter how many of my friends were in there. So instead we cut our losses, ordered in some pizza and consoled ourselves with thoughts of next year when we would be at the party and someone else would be stuck behind the desk.

When my shift finally ended I slumped backstage to the locker room and changed into my civilian clothes. With Eva headed to the after party, I was taking a taxi home. The ballroom festivities had ended over half an hour earlier and at the other wing of the hotel, so I didn't expect to see any of my evening-dress-clad colleagues on my way out.

No sooner had I stepped through the doors than I walked straight into Audrey.

I had met Audrey in my earliest Disney days, back when I was a guest of the hotel and she was in training in the hotel's Food and Beverage department. I'd taken an instant dislike to her, mainly because she was as empty and fake as the Prada handbags my mother brings me back from her vacations. As far as I could tell, Audrey had felt the same way about me. She'd left to work in a restaurant on the other side of the city but since we had a vaguely mutual friend at Front Desk and tended, through no fault of our own, to run into each other on a semi-regular basis, we tried to make nice. You'd never tell we were mutually allergic; when we got together it was like a competition to see who could be the most fake.

She started us off by pretending it was nice to see me, and I pretended that I thought it was okay to dress like Carrie Bradshaw in real life. Just before I was about to choke on my own vomit, Audrey asked me if I was coming along to whatever local bar the after party gang was headed to.

'Actually, I think I'll just go home,' I said. I had already decided to avoid the entire proceedings, not being in the mood for a crowd of the inebriated telling me how great the party I'd hadn't been at had been.

'Oh, really?' Audrey said, acting disappointed. Then she looked my jeans and T-shirt up and down and asked me how I was getting home.

An interesting state of feigned ignorance had settled over Front Desk in the past couple of months. Everyone knew that I didn't drive or own a car, but they also knew that I hated people drawing attention to the fact, feeling sorry for me or offering to help. I certainly didn't want anyone making a big deal of the fact that, sometimes, I had to take a cab home. So I pretended I was fine, they pretended I was fine, and that was fine with me. I let everyone assume that I came in and out every day with Eva, even though we rarely had the same days off and she sometimes worked an earlier shift. No one ever questioned me directly about it.

But Audrey was (a) evil and (b) not Front Desk or even Duck and Tuna anymore, so she couldn't be expected to do the same.

'I'm just going to get a cab,' I said through a tight smile.

Audrey's face fell like a landslide - the drama! 'Really? Oh my God, that's awful. You poor thing. That's really, like, *awful*.'

'It's fine, really. No big deal.'

Right now no one else was around, but if Audrey was here then other people could be too. I was not going to let this fake fest grow in number. I had to get away.

'No, it is really, really awful.' She put a hand over her mouth. 'Poor Catherine!' She stuck out her lower lip for added effect.

'Poor Catherine' assured her that she was absolutely fine and tried to leave.

'Do you want to come with us?' she called after me. 'I could ask around and see if someone would drop you off?'

'No, really.'

'Are you sure? Will you be okay?'

'Absolutely!' By now I was shouting this to her over my shoulder as I hurried away from her and her faux concern. 'It's fine, really. I'll see you later. Enjoy your evening!'

I left her standing there in half an evening dress and with my head down, walked to the Boardwalk in record time where I hopped in a cab. Between missing the Christmas party, having to watch everyone else make their way to it and, last but not least, dealing with Audrey, all I wanted to do now was get home, make a nice cup of tea, crawl into bed with a few episodes of *24* and forget all about this sorry evening.

The apartment looked dark and quiet, my roommates already having retired for the night. I felt in my bag for my door key but couldn't find it. I checked the inner zipped compartment, twice. I patted my jeans pockets, front and back. Finally I knelt on the pavement and upturned my bag, searching through its jumbled contents.

But there was no key.

I knocked at the door. It was late, but not obscenely so, and surely they'd understand that I'd somehow managed to lose my key. While I was at work I hung my clothes in a garment bag in the locker room; the keys had probably been in a pocket and fallen into the bottom of the bag. I'd just pick them up tomorrow.

But there was no answer.

I knocked again.

The irony of this situation was sickening. First of all, I'd been hanging up jeans in a garment bag on average three times a week for the past three months, and my keys had never fallen out before. Secondly, not two nights ago the Papa John's delivery guy had accidentally roused one of my roommates, and she had come wandering out into the living room, half asleep, to see who'd been at the door. But now no amount of thumping, knocking or banging could wake a single one of them, leaving me no choice but to make my way back to the hotel.

Luckily, I had credit on my phone and cash in my pocket; it was not unusual for me to find myself with neither. I called a cab, waited around in the deserted Plantation Park parking lot for it to arrive and then had it take me back to the hotel where, of course, my keys were sitting in the bottom of my garment bag.

I told myself that all I had to do was get one more cab and this stupid night would be over. I decided to grab one from the front of the Duck, as it was too late now for anyone I knew to be around the place and it would save me another trip to the Boardwalk.

There was one valet holding down the fort outside the main doors. I knew his face, but not his name – he was usually the one who collected a list of events from the desk just as I was ending my shift and he was starting his. We had never spoken. I asked him if he could please call me a cab.

'Where are you headed?'

'Plantation Park? It's right off Exit 68 on I-4.'

The valet – his name tag said his name was Lee – mulled this over for a second, glanced at the hotel's empty driveway and then said, 'You don't need to take a cab. I'll drive you home.'

Let's be clear: our valets did not offer guests rides off property, nor were they supposed to leave it during their shifts. But Lee, recognising me from our nightly ten seconds of interaction as I handed him a sheet of paper across the desk, decided to be nice and save me a cab fare. Either that, or he saw by my face how bad an evening I was having and tried to lighten my load. Whatever the motivation, I had no fight left in me to refuse and so I accepted his offer gratefully. He radioed inside to say that he was taking his break a bit early and then he used it to drive me home.

On the short drive there we made small talk about work and missing the Christmas party, and he didn't ask me why I was taking a cab home from work, or why I was leaving the hotel at one in the morning when I'd finished work two hours before. After that night, he never mentioned it on the rare occasions when we passed each other in the halls but after this random act of kindness, I always made sure now to smile and say hi.

I was so grateful for that short ride home.

Predictably, when I finally got inside my apartment that night, out came the waterworks. How much longer could this go on, with me forever teetering on the brink of disaster? The answer wasn't every long at all, because I didn't have the energy. I honestly had no clue what I would have done if I didn't have phone credit or cash, or if I hadn't found the keys at the bottom of that garment bag. In the half darkness I stood in front of my bathroom mirror and took a good long look at my tear-streaked (but tanned) face.

This wasn't what Florida was supposed to be doing with me, and this wasn't what I was supposed to be doing with Florida.

I wanted to be in love with Orlando, the way Eva was. I wanted to be able to pop to Publix for a few groceries in the morning, stop by Starbucks for a coffee, visit Barnes and Noble on my afternoon off, drive to the beach on a sunny Sunday. I wanted to make plans to meet up with my friends without worrying about how I would get there and back. I wanted to live in an apartment that felt like a home, in a place that felt like a neighbourhood, with people I counted among my friends. I wanted a chance to have the Florida life I'd expected.

I wanted a car.

The first of January was less than a fortnight away. I resolved that my New Year's resolution would be to learn to drive and buy a car. I had no idea how I was going to accomplish either of these things, I was just confident that I *would*. The months remaining on my J-1 visa were speedily disappearing; already, I'd wasted nearly four whole months being a miserable, moaning wretch.

I refused to waste another single one.

But first, I had to get through Christmas Day.

By an evil fluke, I had both Christmas Eve (my absolute favourite day of the year) and Christmas Day off work. Although initially my heart sank at the sight of the schedule, I soon realised that this meant I could try and pull off Plan B: staying in bed all day and pretending that it was just your average Thursday. Eva had been invited to have Christmas dinner with her roommate's family, so I was alone in my festive avoidance endeavours. I began to plan accordingly.

Presents had been arriving via international mail for the past two weeks and, for the first time in my life, I'd managed not to open them on contact. Any time a suspected gift appeared in my mailbox, I'd stuff it in my suitcase, snap the padlock closed and stand it in the furthest corner of the closet. I ordered *Elf* from Netflix so I'd have a Christmas movie to watch and bought a headset for my laptop so that I could call everyone back home on Christmas morning.

I tried to picture what Christmas would be like if I were at home in Cork. My brother John, sister Claire and I would all get up really early and race downstairs to open our presents under the tree. Then Claire and I would dispatch John to the kitchen to make us tea and toast.

And so I decided that that was what I wanted: toast. I couldn't remember the last time I'd eaten it. I bought a toaster at the Goodings store down the street from Plantation Park along with a box of imported Barry's tea-bags (made in Cork), a sliced loaf of bread and some half-decent looking butter.

My plan was simple: have my own version of Christmas – tea, toast, *Elf*, presents – on Christmas Eve evening, then sleep through as much of Christmas Day as I possibly could. Taking into account the five-hour time difference, Christmas in Ireland would practically be done and dusted by the time I woke up.

Which is exactly what I did. As soon as it got dark on Christmas Eve, I opened my presents. There was a beautiful necklace, a miniature Christmas cake, a pill box on which a cartoon woman claimed that, 'Being unstable and bitchy is all part of my mystique', and a box of chocolates. Tears sprung to my eyes when I saw that my friend Iain had sent a beaded bag from Paperchase, my favourite store in the entire world. However, in terms of presents, my mother took the grand prize.

A few days before I left for Florida, my mother, brother and I had been wandering around an electronics store when I spotted a bright pink leather laptop bag. It was a thing of pure beauty. Pink is my favourite colour and with its shoulder strap it looked just like a regular, if oversized, handbag. But it was over a hundred euro and I already had a perfectly good (if ugly) laptop bag, so I'd had to leave it in the store behind me.

I'd forgotten all about it, but Mum hadn't.

Here in front of me, amidst shards of bubble-wrap and parcel paper, was the pink leather laptop bag. And just when I thought it couldn't get any better, I opened it to discover it was packed full of Taytos (Irish crisps), Cadbury's Dairy Milk chocolate, a few Weekend *Examiners* (our local newspaper), more Barry's tea-bags, Christmas decorations and cards – a veritable banquet of treats from home.

I sat on the bed admiring the bag, the only bit of colour in the entire room. If I was back home, it would fit right in with my pale pink wallpaper, my scattered pillows, the scarves and bags hanging off my closet doors, but here – here it looked out of place, like it didn't belong.

And neither did I, at least not like this.

It was time to do something about that.

PART II
Good Morning, America!

Nine
MILES IN AMERICA

I needed a car, which meant that I needed money to buy a car, which meant that I needed to ask my parents for money to buy a car.

I spent the first day of January composing a pleading email to send home.

Dear Mum and Dad,
I know it's just after Christmas and everything but time is pressing. How would you feel about loaning me $4,000? Before you freak out, let me explain. If I'm going to stay here then I need to buy a car. You just can't get anywhere without one. There are no footpaths; everything is connected by highway. All my money is going on rent ($600 per month) and cab fare ($250). If I had a car, I could live somewhere cheaper. I know it's a lot of money and I should have saved it up before I came here, but it's a bit late for that now. Let me know.
The Most Expensive One

My mother replied with one of her trademark stream-of-consciousness messages spared, for the most part, the use of grammar or capitalisation.

hi catherine

just read your email!!! a few questions!!! who is going to give you driving lessons and at what cost? how would you know what type of car to buy and not buy a death trap?? your uncle was saying that the americans are all crazy lunatic drivers they drive under the influence of drink and drugs how would you know you wont be a nervous wreck on the road we dont want a call saying youre in hospital with all types of injuries!!! what about your health insurance coverage? doesnt eva drive you to work couldnt she drive you around the shops as well??? your father is saying that you would be better off coming home if its that hard to live out there!!!!!!
love all, mam

I was not impressed. The scope of my predicament was clearly lost on my parental units, so I decided to employ the use of superfluous capital letters to drive my point home, so to speak.

Mum,
Oh my god you two are SUCH psychos. If driving out here is SO dangerous, why does ANYONE do it? I'm NOT coming home just because you need a car to live here. You need a car EVERYWHERE. I can't just live in Holland for the rest of my life because they happen to have a good rail network. And no, Eva CANNOT drive me 'around the shops,' as you put it. I want to be INDEPENDENT, transportation wise at least. I want to LEARN HOW TO DRIVE. I'm already 24 and the longer I leave it the WORSE it will be.
Catherine

While I left my mother and father to consider my (latest) parental loan application, I began apartment hunting with my new friend and soon-to-be roommate, Andrea.

Andrea had started working Duck Front Desk in November, and we'd immediately bonded over our eerily similar prime-time TV viewing habits and love of eye rolling. She was from neighbouring Polk County and had a round trip of ninety minutes to work; she needed to move to Orlando. I needed to get out of Plantation Park – step two of two in my plan to get happy in Florida – so we decided to get an apartment together.

Whenever things were quiet at work we'd scan apartment listings online and interview our co-workers about their neighbourhoods, but it wasn't until the beginning of February that our search got serious. On one of those infrequent days when we both happened to be off, Andrea picked me up in her car and off we went on a tour of Orlando, trying to find ourselves a new apartment.

Andrea was no fool – she wouldn't have ended up paying $600 for a bedroom in Plantation Park, let me tell you – so I was perfectly happy to let her do all the talking while I committed the floor plans of potential bedrooms to memory for decorating purposes. By the end of the day, we had narrowed it down to two contenders.

The first was a ground floor unit in Broadwater, a short distance from Sea World on International Drive. It ticked all the boxes: two-bed/two-bath; washer/dryer; ample parking, and only a ten-minute drive to the doors of the hotel. The complex had a small gym and two pleasant pool areas, our patio offered a view of Sea World's nightly fireworks and our friend and co-worker Ted had lived in Broadwater for the past year without complaint. Unfortunately, the rent was at the top of our budget.

Our other option seemed too good to be true. Not far from the swanky Mall at Millennia, we found Oak Springs, a small apartment complex on Conroy Road. We pulled in after spotting a huge banner hanging outside advertising available units. Again the unit and the complex met all our requirements, although I was a tad nervous about having to use the interstate to get to work every day. After our second golf-cart ride of the afternoon, the leasing agent, Courtney, brought us back to the clubhouse and the hard sell began.

Oak Springs had recently come under new ownership, Courtney explained, and was in the process of being completely refurbished. This would mean that our potential apartment would be, for all intents and purposes, brand new: freshly laid flooring, appliances just out of the box, paint barely dry. She pulled out a colour wheel and told us that, as a 'moving-in present,' we could choose a shade for an accent wall in our living room. If that wasn't enough, the complex was also offering new tenants one month's rent completely free. Since we didn't have a television or a couch – and I didn't even have a *bed* – this would go a long way to fattening up our furniture fund and reducing the number of nights I'd be forced to sleep on the air mattress I'd borrowed from Eva.

Initially, Andrea and I had the same reaction: we wanted to know how soon we could move in. But the more we thought about it, the more we realised it all sounded a bit suspicious. So we turned to the apartment hunters' fair-weather friend, ApartmentRatings.com.

Apartment Ratings is to apartment complexes what Trip Advisor is to hotels and resorts – a place for the angry, bitter and scorned to vent their frustration. Former tenants warned potential new ones about rodent problems, patchy maintenance and loud neighbours, and all the other important things that your friendly leasing agent wasn't going to tell you. It was here we learned the reason behind Oak Spring's distinct odour of desperation: cockroaches.

Living in Central Florida, it wasn't unusual to cross paths with the odd roach. But there's a considerable difference between a single cockroach scuttling across the floor and having several generations of them multiplying under your sink, running all over your countertops, falling from the ceiling onto your bed while you're asleep or flying around your living room in swarms – all experiences we could expect to enjoy if we took up residence in Oak Springs, at least according to the angry posts on Apartment Ratings. Just as we'd suspected, Oak Springs and its promises were simply too good to be true, so it was back to Broadwater.

We paid a second visit to their clubhouse to see if we could broker a better deal, but they refused to budge on the monthly rent, the security deposit or the 'processing fee' we'd have to pay just to apply for a lease. But after our Oak Springs debacle, we now saw the merit in this. Broadwater didn't need us – if we didn't take the apartment, someone else would. We filled out an application, I handed over photocopies of my passport and J-1 visa, and we celebrated our decision with a venti no-foam latte (me) and a grande non-fat caramel macchiato (Andrea) in what might soon be our local Starbucks.

But if we were approved for the Broadwater apartment, I'd be marooned there unless I had a car and, fairly crucially, I knew how to drive it.

I wasn't the biggest fan of driving. Actually, I *hated* the idea of being responsible for a vehicle that could potentially kill someone, as that was sure to be the first thing I'd do. If you're familiar with the scene in *Clueless* where Dionne accidentally drives onto the freeway, takes both hands off the wheel and starts screaming hysterically, then you'll have some idea of what I feared I'd be like behind the wheel. There was just so much to think about: the clutch; the gears; the accelerator; the brakes; the disc changer – and on top of all that, you had to concentrate on where you were going as well. I thought I'd never manage it. Until one day, en route to work, I happened to glance over at Eva and notice for the first time that she was driving with just one leg.

For one hour many years ago, an ex-boyfriend of mine had taken me out for a driving lesson in the worst possible place to learn how to drive: Cork's barrier-free docklands, where one accidental depress of the accelerator would have put both of us in a watery grave. Under such intense pressure I had been barely able to sit still in the driver's seat, let alone operate the car. The lesson had ended abruptly when *someone* failed to explain to me the correct way to change gears and the engine almost exploded.

After that, I had vowed I would never try again. Driving just seemed awfully complicated. So how now was Eva doing it with just one foot?

'It's an automatic,' she said. 'You just press the accelerator when you want to go, and the brake when you want to stop.'

'You mean there's no clutch?'

'Of course there's no clutch – it's an automatic!'

What did I think automatic meant? To be honest, I hadn't really thought much about it. I suppose I'd assumed it meant that you didn't manually change gears, but knowing next to nothing about cars I hadn't connected this with no clutch action either.

This changed everything. Assuaged by this new information, driving lessons commenced the next day.

I met Eva and her 1996 Oldsmobile outside her apartment. Her car was long, wide and squat, with a handbrake where I thought the windscreen wipers lever should be. Parking it was, for me, like trying to manoeuvre a flatbed truck whilst blindfolded. It wasn't the perfect car to learn how to drive on, but Eva was the perfect instructor. Calm almost to the point of nonchalance, she was utterly convinced that I would not – *could* not – crash her car, and had not a single qualm about letting me drive it despite my being inept, uninsured and non-licensed. Nor did she worry about my killing us both in a fiery car accident, even though it was all I could think about.

Eva parked the car in the middle of Plantation Park's perimeter road and we swapped seats with the engine running. After checking three times that we were both belted in, I tentatively took hold of the wheel and Eva released the handbrake. The car began to inch forward.

I gently pressed the accelerator until we were going about twenty miles an hour. I may have been on the verge of hyperventilating and my knuckles were already white, but I *was* driving, albeit at a pace a snail could exceed. We circled the complex a few times and tried a few stops and starts. I even reversed a little bit. An hour or so later, I nudged the car into a parking space (that had a free space on either side, just in case) and despite my being askew by about forty-five degrees, the lesson was deemed a success.

Half an hour passed before I could unfurl my claw-like fingers.

With the basic operations down it was now time to practice on real roads, so Eva and I started touring Disney World late at night. A learner driver's dream, Disney property has miles upon miles of two and three lane highways with traffic lights, intersections, exit ramps and – gulp – merge lanes, that are all practically deserted after midnight. Slowly but surely, over the course of a couple of weeks, my terror began to fade and confidence took its place.

No one was killed or injured, but it wasn't all plain sailing. One night a possum darted into the middle of the road in front of me, forcing me to bring the car to a sudden, screeching halt. The possum lived to tell the tale, Eva commended me on my emergency stop, and I chose not to point out that if there had been another vehicle behind us, we'd have been burning our backsides on its headlights. Another time, I was carefully making my way down an exit ramp bordered on both sides by a five foot drop to a swampy ditch when the car unexpectedly passed through some sprinklers, showering the windscreen with water in a loud and sudden shock and switching me to panic mode. I had never had to work the wipers before and now, anytime I diverted attention to finding them, the car veered dangerously to the left. I was about to have a *Clueless* moment when Eva reached across and flipped them on, saving us from an unscheduled trip into green stagnant water.

Then came the ultimate test: driving all the way home from work. This ten-minute journey held all sorts of horrors for the learner driver: State Road 536, merging onto Interstate 4 and a busy four-way intersection. When Eva first proposed it, I thought she was kidding. We were, after all, too young to die.

Less than three weeks after I'd first driven Eva's car, I slowly pulled the Oldsmobile out of the hotel parking lot and very, *very* carefully started on the journey home. Eva directed me in and out of lanes and said things like, 'Okay, Catherine. There's a gigantic bus about to pull up alongside you, so don't freak out.' All was going well until the time came to merge left onto the mayhem of the I-4 (actually pretty quiet at that time of night but I had no frame of reference) and Eva's cell phone rang.

To my horror she answered it, leaving me to get us the rest of the way home without any help.

I tried to breathe deeply and remain calm. *You can do this*, I told myself. *Even Britney Spears can drive.* I could see the end of the ramp ahead and the beginning of I-4, alight with cars streaking past in both directions. Any second now and we'd both be in the danger zone. Eva was happily chatting away on her phone and looking out the passenger window, oblivious to her imminent dance with death. Once the exit lane spat me out onto the Interstate, I'd have about ten seconds to get over to the left or I'd run out of road.

Okay. Here we go.

I checked the rear-view mirror, both side mirrors and then turned around in my seat to look back, just in case. The way seemed clear. As long as everybody stayed where they were, I'd be okay. The car behind me put on its indicator. I put on mine. Deep breath. It was now or never. I looked behind me one last time before I gripped the wheel and swung it counter-clockwise. My life flashed before my eyes – five years old, eight years old, twelve years old - along with the lights of the other cars switching lanes at speed all around me but then-

We're alive! And in the right lane! Oh, joy! I can breathe again.

But only for half a minute. We had joined I-4 after Exit 67 and we needed to leave it again at Exit 68. Signs were already urging me to move back to the right and into the Exit Only lane that had appeared.

Getting off I-4 was even worse because faster, more confident and most likely licensed drivers were overtaking me and moving into the exit lane. Once again, I checked all my mirrors, turned to look behind and with only seconds to spare, moved to the right ahead of the car behind me.

I had done it - I had survived I-4! I had driven on the interstate and lived to tell the tale. I slowed down on the ramp and came to a stop at a red light, thankful for the opportunity to catch my breath. Only metres beyond this intersection was the entrance to Plantation Park. My ordeal was almost over.

Just as the lights changed, Eva hung up on her telephone conversation. She started to fill me in on the latest Front Office gossip, then suddenly she stopped and said, 'Oh my God! I totally forgot you were driving!'

Despite being on the verge of passing out, I just shrugged and said, 'It's okay. I was totally fine. Not a problem.'

'You can drive!' Eva proclaimed, clapping. 'You can drive!'

With my pulse threatening to beat its way out of my neck, I nodded in agreement.

Meanwhile a week after we submitted our application, Andrea and I were approved as Broadwater leaseholders, and Moving In Day was set for seven days time. I had driven Eva and I home from work every night for a week and was growing evermore confident that, one day soon, I would be able to change lanes without a spotter. At the age of twenty-four I had finally learned to

117

drive (an automatic, but still). All I needed to do now was buy a car.

I thought the hardest part was over.

I was very, *very* wrong.

Before I could apply for a learner's permit, I had to take the Drugs, Alcohol and Traffic Awareness, or DATA Test. Just like everything else stateside, the matter could be taken care of online. I downloaded the Florida Driver's Handbook in PDF format and took the DATA course in four hour-long modules, followed by the test. Questions included such brainteasers as, 'Alcohol impairs your judgment: true or false?' My debit card was charged $29.95, and two days later my DATA certificate arrived in the mail. Worryingly, I'd learned the rules of the road without leaving the living room.

After some, ahem, *wrangling*, my parents had agreed to finance the purchase of a car. Putting aside a security deposit for Broadwater, the price of a new bed, car insurance and a small rainy day fund, I had about $2,000 to spend on my first ever motorised vehicle.

The universe seemed to be responding to my new positive outlook. Miho's work visa was set to expire any day now, and she happened to have a car she needed to get rid of before she returned to Japan. It was a white 1998 Mitsubishi Mirage, a cute little four-door about half the length and width of Eva's Oldsmobile, with about 115,000 miles on the clock. Oh, and an oil leak. The Mirage was famous around the hotel following an incident involving Miho, a pig and the middle of I-95.

High mileage, an oil leak and a previous accident; it was perfect.

I had looked online, mainly on Autotrader and Craigslist, but hadn't seen anything for less than three thousand dollars that wasn't being sold for parts. I couldn't really go to a dealership because of the headaches my status as a non-resident alien with only a learner's permit would undoubtedly cause, not to mention my absolutely non-existent knowledge of car bits. I could look under the hood of a car and not notice that the engine was missing, and that was if I managed to get the hood up in the first place.

I had been advised by various impartial people that the Mirage wasn't too bad a deal and that it would last me another year without any major repair or expense. Miho presented me with a sheaf of maintenance records and receipts that not only assured me everything was in working order, but also suggested that she was suffering from the car owner's version of Munchausen's by proxy; every time the Mirage as much as spluttered, Miho rushed it to the mechanic. One of the receipts said, 'customer reports car makes unusual noise when turning corners.'

Miho suggested I take it for a test drive so one afternoon, with my move to Broadwater only days away, Eva, Miho and I met in the parking lot of Dolly Parton's Dixie Stampede on Vineland Avenue.

As soon as I sat into the driver's seat I knew the car was mine. Miho had kept the interior in excellent condition, the handbrake was in a more familiar location between the two front seats, and there was plenty of space for shopping bags in the trunk. There were even two cupholders – one for my latte and one for the caramel macchiato I'd be bringing home for Andrea. In an amazing and somewhat suspicious coincidence, Miho's asking price was exactly what I had to spend - $2,000 – and even though she wasn't really in a position to make demands, she wouldn't budge on the money. But I liked the car and I didn't want to have to go to a dealership, so I told her I'd take it.

Miho needed it for a few more days while she tied up her loose ends in Orlando, and so we arranged to meet in three days time to exchange the car and its title documents for cash. The plan was that Eva would then bring me to the DMV for my learner's permit, to her insurance company for a policy and then back to the DMV for my licence plate and registration. I'd have a few days to get used to driving the Mirage before I'd fill it full of my stuff and move ten minutes away to my sparkly new apartment in Broadwater.

Every part of my master plan had fallen into place.

Or so I thought.

Miho called the following morning and said we needed to talk.

'I don't think I can sell you my car,' was all she would say over the phone.

Miho, if you couldn't already tell by her Front Desk notebook and her unnecessary visits to the mechanic, was a tad highly strung. Even making the smallest, most mundane everyday decision took a lot out of her. Since finishing up with work, she had been visiting the hotel, making sure she got a photo with and bid farewell to everyone on her list. And there was an *actual* list: a Front Office schedule highlighting – with an *actual* highlighter – the people she had already bade good-bye. As Claire, one of my managers, had once said, 'Being Miho must be *exhausting.*'

I suspected that Miho had been thinking non-stop about the terms of our deal, had come across some miniscule discrepancy or flaw and panicked. But no matter what it was I was confident I could talk her back around.

I arranged to meet her that night at the Virgin Megastore café in Downtown Disney. Miho arrived a minute late and then spent the next five apologising for it. When she was done, I asked her why she had suddenly decided that she couldn't sell me her car.

'Well...' She looked at the floor. 'I was talking to one of my friends, and they said that if I sold you the car and you crashed the car and you hurt or killed somebody when you crashed the car, that person's family could sue me because I sold you the car even though I knew that you did not have a licence.'

This was exactly the sort of unlikely event Miho lay awake at night worrying about, so I couldn't say I was surprised. I was, however, interested in finding out who this friend was, so I could throttle them for messing up my Mirage deal. They should have known that Miho was terrified of litigation-happy Americans.

I explained as best I could that this scenario could not transpire. After Miho transferred the title to my name the car was no longer hers, and therefore whoever was driving it was no longer her responsibility.

As she seemed to digest this I thought that maybe the crazy fog had lifted and the road to my new car was clear. But then Miho took something from her bag that might have been the most disturbing thing I have ever seen in my life, before or since. Even as I was reeling from the shock of it I was already thinking, *no one is going to believe this when I tell them about it later.*

It was a chart, drawn on a piece of letter-sized paper in Miho's distinct, neat handwriting. My name was at the top of one of the columns. Even reading it upside down I could tell that this was the problem - Miho had gone to the trouble of *constructing a chart* of all the reasons she couldn't sell me her car.

Realising this was going to be a long night, I ordered another large latte and over the next hour, argued every one of Miho's unfounded concerns into irrelevancy. We brokered a deal, beat by beat, that would transfer the Mirage's ownership in a way that would cancel out all of Miho's legal worries. It went like this:

First thing Friday morning she would bring the car to Plantation Park and remove her licence plate. I'd have $2,000 in cash ready and waiting to exchange for the keys. Eva would drive both of us to the DMV on Bronson Highway where I'd get my temporary permit and Miho would have me sign a Bill of Sale and the title, so she could prove twice over that she had sold me the car.

Then all three of us would visit Eva's insurance company and, with my learner's permit and the car's title, I would take out a policy. After that it would be back to the DMV where my licence, title and proof of insurance would enable me to register the car in my name and get a licence plate. Finally, I'd return to Plantation Park and put the plate on my new car.

Miho added this step-by-step transfer procedure to her chart and studied it for holes.

'Who owns the car while it is parked outside your apartment?' she wanted to know.

I asked why in the world that would matter.

'It is illegal to have a car without a licence plate. Maybe the police will drive by while we are all at the DMV and see the car with no licence plate. They will think the car is stolen, and take it away. Who will be responsible? You will have given me the money, but the car will still be in my name.'

I silently counted to ten and reminded myself that although it may not look like it now, this was actually going to be easier than trying to buy a car from a dealership.

'I think that's very unlikely,' I said evenly. 'First of all, unless someone calls them, the police will not be driving around Plantation Park. And we can reverse the car into the space, so no one will even know it doesn't have a licence plate.'

Miho didn't look convinced. As our meeting approached the two-hour mark and she still hadn't agreed to go ahead with the sale, my well of saintly patience abruptly ran dry.

'Look,' I snapped, unable to hide my irritation any longer, 'I'm moving to a new apartment in three days. If you can't sell me your car then tell me now, because I'll need to start looking for another one.'

I don't enjoy confrontations and I especially don't enjoy them with people I consider to be my friends. But *two hours* of back and forth over the sale of a stupid car? I just couldn't take it anymore. Miho looked hurt, so I quickly added that I was sorry for snapping at her but even she had to admit that this was getting ridiculous. Every hour of every day, people were swapping cars for money and they certainly didn't spend hours and hours working out every last detail of the exchange. I was already appeasing Miho by letting her tag along with me to the DMV when all she needed to do was to drop the car and title off at my place and leave with her money and her licence plate.

I felt like the parent saving a place at the dinner table for little Suzy's imaginary friend.

'That's not the problem,' Miho said finally. 'I can't sell you the car because I think you are irresponsible.'

Excuse me?

Now; I hadn't seen *that* coming.

'What,' I said, trying to stay calm, 'are you talking about?'

'You drove Eva's car without a licence and you were not insured on it at the time. You told me yourself you even drove on I-4 in it. How do I know you will not drive my car without a licence or insurance?'

This time I counted to twenty. 'Well, for one thing, it won't be *your car.*'

Miho said nothing.

'And a couple of days ago, you let me drive your car too.'

'I know.' Her face was filled with regret. 'I shouldn't have done that. It was very irresponsible of me.'

'Miho...' I tried to think of sentences that weren't filled with expletives. 'You are creating problems where there are none. You'll be with me at the DMV and you'll be with me at the insurance place. You'll see for yourself that by the time I sit in that car I'll be licensed and insured and by then it won't be your car anyway.' *So get over it.*

'But what if you can't get insurance because you only have a per-'

'Then Eva will sign as the primary driver.'

'But what if Eva leaves before you–'

'Then Andrea will do it'.

'But what if–'

I threw up my hands, exasperated. 'This is crazy, do you understand? You are being *crazy*.' I drew circles on my temple, the official international hand gesture for a few beers short of a six-pack, to demonstrate my point. 'This does not have to be so complicated. All you're doing is selling me your car, okay? I just cannot talk about this anymore or my head will explode. Either we do it like we said on Friday, or we don't do it at all.'

She said nothing.

'What'll be?' I started picking up my discarded sugar packets to show her I meant business. It was a risky bluff.

'Okay,' she said, after some thought. 'I will sell you my car.'

'Thanks.'

I got up and left.

After negotiations of UN magnitude, I had finally convinced Miho to let me pay her two thousand dollars to take her excuse for a car (that had once killed a pig) off her hands the day before she had to leave the country.

After all this trouble, the damn thing had better last me a year.

Friday morning, Eva and I braced ourselves for Mission Mirage.

Miho brought the car to Plantation Park, backed it into a space and removed the licence plate. On the drive to the DMV, Eva and Miho made awkward small talk while I held my breath.

When we got there, Miho asked the desk clerk for a Bill of Sale.

'You don't need one of those,' the clerk said dismissively.

'But I want one,' Miho retorted.

'But you don't *need* one.'

'But I want one,' Miho said again.

The clerk looked to me for help. 'We know it's unnecessary,' I said. 'But she would like to have one for her records.'

The clerk gave me a look that said she too had been saving places at the table for imaginary friends, and went off to get one. Miho and I both signed it, and I took a copy for appearances.

By late afternoon, when we dropped Miho off at the hotel to make some more progress with her goodbye list, I think even she had begun to realise that she'd completely overreacted and blown what should have been a simple transaction out of all logical proportion. But I could forgive her now because she had, in the end, sold me her car.

The next morning I woke up in a new Orlando.

I doubt Willy Shakespeare himself could convey how it felt for me to finally have a car. I could drive to the grocery store and pick things off the shelves with abandon, now that I didn't have to worry about carrying them home. Hell, I could fill a cart with bricks if I wanted to – I'd still be able to haul them back to my apartment. I could drive to Starbucks and get a coffee. I could drive to Barnes and Noble and buy books. I could drive to Target and buy a cute bedspread. I could drive to the mall and buy – well, anything really.

I could drive to my new apartment in Broadwater. I could drive from there to work and back. I could arrange to meet my friends wherever and whenever, without worrying about how to get there. I could go explore – Celebration, Kennedy Space Centre, Cocoa Beach.

Every day was suddenly threatening to burst with the possibilities that driving added to them.

Dear Mum and Dad,

You will be pleased to know that I am now the proud owner of a 1998 Mitsubishi Mirage DE 4-door sedan. I am fully insured against all eventualities [a lie: I had the bare legal minimum which only protected the State against any damage I caused] *and I will never drive alone; as per the regulations of a learner's permit, Eva or Andrea will accompany me at all times* [if they're available, otherwise I'll just chance it]. *The average speed limit is sixty miles an hour and I never go over fifty unless I'm overtaking* [or Metallica's 'Fuel' is playing – that song always makes me want to drive really fast]. *Andrea and I move into our new apartment on Tuesday so my rent goes down by nearly $150 a month* [but now I have utilities which average $100 a month]; *I can buy cheaper groceries* [but now I'll be spending a lot more money on frivolous things just because I can drive to the store that sells them] *and I never have to pay for a cab again* [but I do have to buy gas]. *Having a car has completely changed my life here in Florida. Thanks so much for helping me!*

The Most Expensive One

hi catherine,

well thats great!!! drive safe and be careful watch out for all those drunk americans on drugs!!!! always look around before changing lanes and put on your indicator even if theres no one else around!!! when are you taking your test???

love all, mam

p.s. dad was surprised to hear they still use miles in america!! aren't they a little slow to catch on over there??!

Ten
MISSION SPACE

March was a beautiful month to be in Central Florida. With no stifling heat or humidity to speak of, most afternoons managed to get from beginning to end without a single drop of rain.

I had been living in Orlando for a full six months now and, if you forgot almost everything that had happened during the first five of them, then you could have made yourself a nice little montage of me and put it to that 'Time of My Life' tune from *Dirty Dancing*. Catherine driving her new car. Catherine waking up in her new apartment. Catherine lounging by the pool. Catherine buying more stuff she doesn't need in the Super Target on 192. Catherine going for a drink with her friends on a Wednesday night. Catherine and Andrea bitching about work on their patio late into the evening. I had even chopped off all my straw-like blonde hair and opted instead for a neat brunette bob, because every new beginning needs a new haircut to go with it and no matter what I did I couldn't get my long locks straight.

The only dip in my recent trajectory of escalating joy was Eva's departure. She had decided to finish up her J-1 program early and resume her studies in Canada. After a farewell night with what seemed like half the hotel at good old Buffalo Wild Wings, I said goodbye with the gifts of a photo of us on Main Street framed in Mickey's silhouette and a list of one hundred movies I insisted she watch immediately, if only so that she could understand the vast majority of pop culture references. Whatever Eva had got from her second stint in Orlando, I knew what she had done for me and that was nothing short of everything. She had been my friend, taught me to drive and shown me that living in Orlando could be fun. We were practically a Disney movie waiting to happen.

But there was one important thing that I still hadn't done, an apple I'd yet to pluck from my newfound tree of Floridian happiness.

I still hadn't been to Kennedy Space Centre.

In a childhood filled with fleeting obsessions, America's National Aeronautics and Space Administration (NASA) had managed to maintain a strong and constant footing in the foreground of my mind.

Or at least the Space Shuttle had, anyway.

I had no time for Apollo, the programme that appeared to have had stuffed three men into a dinky tin can, shot them into space, slung them around the moon and dragged them back home again. When I was eight years old and leafing through my *Footprints* history textbook, I had come across the story of the *Apollo 11* lunar landing and decided that I wanted to be an astronaut. But then over the page I had seen a photo of the crew capsule, charred and blackened by the heat of re-entry, bobbing on the surface of the ocean awaiting rescue and promptly changed my mind back again.

One idle afternoon not long after, I discovered the movie *Space Camp* on the shelves of my local video store. Set at the very real NASA summer camp in Huntsville, Alabama, this implausible adventure begins when a team of kids is accidentally launched into space aboard a runaway Shuttle which is, of course, something that could *totally* happen in real life. In order to get safely back home they have to work together, forge friendships, realise that they are more alike than they are different and risk an EVA (that's Extra Vehicular Activity, or a space walk) to get a couple of oxygen tanks from a make-believe space station called Daedalus. You can guess how the story ends. Watching it, I was mesmerised by the pale, sleek beauty of the Orbiter floating above an iridescent earth, although decidedly unimpressed with the electroshock perm of a teenage Kelly Preston.

I thought the launch of a Space Shuttle was a wondrous thing. On ignition, its engines release a curtain of tiny sparks, before the vehicle – which looks more like an airplane than a spaceship - appears to alight with monstrous flames and ascend to the heavens atop a thick column of white smoke, taking only eight minutes to carry its astronaut crew into space.

Fourteen years passed and other dreams came and went. Then I found myself living less than sixty miles from the launch pads and the Kennedy Space Centre (KSC) Visitor Complex that had since sprung up around them.

Four weeks into my driving life, I decided I had had sufficient practice to make the trip out to Cape Canaveral.

Just after eight o'clock on the morning of March 14th, I pulled out of Broadwater in my little Mirage and hit the long, straight road baked white in the sun that would bring my car and I all the way to the coast.

Today was sure to be an emotional day, and not just because – as I think I've already proved - I tended to cry at the drop of a hat. Florida had finally made friends with me and today was the proof. Seeing the Cape for the first time would be like visiting an amusement park built just for me, a reminder of how living in Florida could be so much fun. I would be treading on the same asphalt as my astronaut heroes once had; I would be able to reach out and touch the black tiles of an Orbiter; my brand new credit card could be put to good use in the Space Shop, the largest store of its kind in the world. Knowing that one, let alone all, of these wonders would be likely to bring about tears or at least childlike excitement, I had thought it best to make this pilgrimage on my own and minimise the embarrassment. Besides, Eva was gone and I wasn't really interested in going to KSC with anyone who had lived in Central Florida all their life and yet had never been.

That just didn't say *enthusiasm* to me.

The night before my trip may as well have been Christmas Eve for all the sleep I got, so my first stop en route was my beloved Starbucks in the Premium Outlet mall. I stuck the first of three newly minted driving CDs into the stereo and eagerly joined the early morning traffic headed for the airport. According to MapQuest, the journey to KSC should take just under an hour, or about forty-five minutes longer than any single drive I had done before. I tried not to think about that, or the fact that driving alone on a learner's permit could lose me my licence.

An hour, two CDs and three toll plazas later, I took a right turn onto State Road 405 and caught sight of the iconic Vehicle Assembly Building (VAB) on the horizon, beyond a shimmering stretch of the Indian River.

On came the waterworks.

The only other time I'd seen the VAB in real life was from the window of the 747 that had brought me to Florida, back when my Mickey Mouse-shaped cup was overflowing with Disney excitement. It had proven to be a rocky few months, but now I finally felt like I was on my feet.

It was a full circle moment, as Oprah likes to say.

I nearly ran the car off the road when I spotted a

Space Shuttle parked up ahead, but it turned out to be merely the scale model advertising the Astronaut Hall of Fame – AKA the poor man's KSC – which I was planning to hit on the way back home.

After a bridge that carried me over the river, I found myself on official NASA soil. One sign welcomed me to KENNEDY SPACE CENTRE: AMERICA'S SPACEPORT (*squeal!*) while a second one warned me that the threat level was elevated (so no change there then).

Parking lots were still a bit nerve-wracking for me, but because I'd arrived early on a weekday morning in March, there were plenty of open spaces. Adorably, each section of the lot was named after a NASA astronaut, so I left the car with Wally Shirra and skipped up to the ticket booths, which I think were supposed to look like the International Space Station (ISS); the solar panels keeping ticket buyers in the shade while they waited. After purchasing a KSC Commander's Club Annual Pass – are you jealous? - and passing through the metal detectors and bag search that post 9/11 America seems to love so damn much, I was finally in and standing in the middle of a large, open plaza.

The blue NASA logo was everywhere and I could see the tops of the Rocket Garden's exhibits over the buildings to my left. My eyes came to rest on The Space Shop directly across from me and my credit card began to beat as if it had a pulse. No doubt my NASA shopping spree would be the highlight of the day, so it was best to leave it for last if I could.

Can I?

Turning my head away from The Space Shop's spoils, I consulted my park map. The KSC Visitor Complex has two main attractions for the entertainment of the space enthusiast and the occasional Discovery Channel watcher alike. There's the Complex itself, with its IMAX theatre, exhibits and not long from now, a brand new amusement ride, and then there's the bus tour which drives you through NASA's history, making three stops along the way: the Launch Pad 39 Viewing Gantry, the Apollo/Saturn V (V as in the Roman numeral for *five*) Centre and the ISS Centre. The route also offers close-up views of NASA's operations, including the Orbiter Processing Facility (OPF) where the Shuttles are prepared for flight, and the aforementioned VAB.

Have you had enough space-related acronyms yet? No? Good.

I hopped on the first bus. With my camera at the ready, we pulled out of the Visitor Complex. Our smiling, middle-aged tour guide narrated our journey and the small video screens onboard explained everything that happens at KSC, taking us through a Shuttle mission from beginning to end.

A large part of the complex was under construction. As well as a multi-million dollar refurbishment, KSC was getting its first ever thrill ride, the Space Shuttle Launch Simulation Facility, which was scheduled to open in the summer. In the meantime, signs asked visitors to 'pardon the space dust'. And all this with money generated solely from ticket sales and donations – not a single taxpayer dollar was spent on the visitor facilities at KSC.

Our driver took us into the 'restricted area' and slowly around the VAB. We all craned our necks against the windows trying to get a good look at it.

Back when the VAB was under construction in the early 1960s, *Life* magazine sent a photographer down to the Cape to capture its size on film. He returned empty-handed. No matter how hard you tried, even your own eyes couldn't fathom the true scale of this monolith, let alone a camera lens.

So let's try some statistics instead.

At the time of its completion, the VAB was the largest manmade structure on earth in terms of volume. More than forty years later, it's still the third largest. At 525 feet, it's the highest point in the State of Florida. It takes forty-five minutes for each of the VAB's four doors to fully retract and the United Nations building could easily fit through any one of them. An American flag is painted on one side; a Greyhound bus could drive down any one of its stripes with room to spare.

It is simply *gargantuan*.

One of the doors was partially open as we passed, and through the gap I could see the tail end of a Solid Rocket Booster (SRB). Right at that moment, the Space Shuttle *Atlantis* was inside undergoing repairs following a freak hailstorm that had damaged the nose of its External Fuel Tank (ET – not EFT, if you were guessing) while it was sitting on the very launch pad we were headed towards now.

To our left was the Crawler Way, along which the launch vehicle – the combination of an Orbiter or Space Shuttle, a rust-coloured ET and two white SRBs, if everyone's still with me – is carefully moved to the launch pad at speeds of less than a mile an hour on top of a purpose-built machine that looks like four tanks linked together: the Crawler Transporter.

Along the Crawler Way to the right was our first stop; the Launch Complex 39 Viewing Gantry, where I watched a short film about Shuttle launches before climbing the stairs to get a better look. Unfortunately, a launch pad isn't very exciting when there's nothing on it – just a tower of grey steel, a lightning rod, and some cables – so I can't say I was overly impressed.

In recent weeks – since my new car had led me to pass many an afternoon in the 'Space' section of my local Barnes and Noble – my NASA obsession had undergone a bit of a paradigm shift, and my admiration for the Space Shuttle program had begun to dwindle.

In its place, I was filled with awe at the glorious Apollo era, which I had started to understand was a far greater feat then slingshotting a can of man around the moon. In fact, the more I learned about it, the more I considered it to be the single most impressive thing ever achieved by the human race.

On September 12th, 1962, President John F. Kennedy dedicated the new NASA Manned Spacecraft Centre near Houston, Texas. Sixteen months earlier he had announced to Congress his conviction that the United States 'should commit itself, before this decade is out, to landing a man on the moon and returning him safely to earth.'

Before the Soviets do it.

Two of the world's biggest superpowers were locked in a race to space and, as the end of the decade approached, the US was lagging behind. Although the Soviet approach to space travel was generally haphazard, risky and held together with duct tape, it *worked* – so far, they could lay claim to the first man in space, the first woman in space and the first space-walk. All that was really left for NASA was to take the first footstep on the surface of the moon.

But that wouldn't be easy.

Some people at NASA weren't even sure it was possible.

For starters, man had never travelled anywhere near that far into space before. NASA Astronauts Dick Gordon and Pete Conrad held the distance record – 850 vertical miles above the earth on *Gemini 12* – which was great and all, but the moon was another 249,150 miles away after that. It would take a three-man crew three days to get there and another three to get back – if they *could* get back, but that was a whole other problem – which meant that NASA would have to launch a crew module they could all fit in, a lunar module with which to land on the moon, as well as somewhere to store enough oxygen, fuel, food and water to keep everyone onboard alive and well for the mission's duration.

The weight of all this couldn't reach orbit on any of NASA's existing rocketry, so a new, more powerful 'moonrocket' would have to be designed and built. This rocket would then launch the entire thing – crew module, service module, lunar module – into a 'parking orbit' 116 miles above the earth. Three hours later, or twice around, the crew would re-ignite the third stage or last part of their massive rocket and head off towards the moon at a speed of approximately 24,000 miles per hour. This manoeuvre was called Translunar Injection, or TLI. Six thousand miles after that, the delicate lunar module or LEM (for Lunar Excursion Module, more commonly called 'the Lem,'), its skin thinner in places than a single sheet of tinfoil, would be taken out, turned around and docked with the Command and Service Module, or CSM, in an intricate weightless ballet that had no room for error. For the next three days, the crew would drift through the blackness of space until they were captured, some 30,000 miles out, by the moon's gravity and pulled the rest of the way there. They would have to time it so that they arrived just as the moon itself, orbiting at speeds of around 2,000 miles an hour, was arriving too, and quickly nudge in front of it. Sixty-nine nautical miles above the moon's surface, the crew would then attempt Lunar Orbit Insertion (LOI) which does exactly what it says on the tin, and once everything had been checked and was reported to be in good working order, two of our three spacemen would climb into the LEM and fly down to the lunar surface, leaving one behind in the CSM to twiddle his thumbs until they were finished.

But the LEM couldn't land just anywhere. It had to aim for the landing spot recommended by NASA's brainiest brain-boxes – and do it with a computer that can't add two numbers together - or risk heading straight for a bottomless crater or a field of jagged boulders. If they did manage to land safely, the crew could get out and stretch their legs for a bit before getting back into the LEM and taking off. If they *could* take off; the ascent engine had no redundancy. It would either work, or it wouldn't. If it does work, the crew would then have to fly back up to the CSM's orbit, catch it as it passed by and reconnect both modules before all three men – and, fingers crossed, some lunar rocks – could embark on the quarter of a million mile journey back home. Once they reached us, they'd aim for the one tiny dot on the earth's surface through which they could safely re-enter, dropping like a stone through the atmosphere at a speed of 24,000 miles an hour and, don't forget, *on fire*, after which they'd hopefully drop slowly to the surface of the ocean and wait patiently for a helicopter ride back to dry land.

Well, that's if the parachutes opened, of course.

At NASA headquarters in Washington D.C., the joke had been that the only real challenge JFK had set them was the 'safely' part. They were pretty sure they could get a man on the moon, but not without risking his life before, during and afterwards. The task was mammoth, riddled with complications and not helped by the seemingly impossible end-of-decade deadline. It's difficult to imagine it now, all these years later and from the advantage of a technologically advanced time, but NASA was trying to go to the moon in the face of total ignorance.

Nobody knew if man could even *survive* in space for that length of time – some of medicine's leading minds postulated that all three astronauts would be long dead from radiation poisoning before they even caught sight of the moon.

One NASA think tank even suggested sending a man to the moon as soon as possible and leaving him up there until they figured out a way to get him back. At least this way, they'd be sure to make their deadline *and* beat the Russians.

But somehow they solved the problem. Four hundred thousand of America's brightest minds (and a rather famous one of Germany's, rocket genius Werner Von Braun) put their brainy heads together and figured it all out. While the astronauts were the public face of the space program, posing with their wives for *Life* magazine covers and cutting the ribbons of new car dealerships,

NASA's army of physicists, engineers and mathematicians worked from dusk 'til dawn in back rooms across the country to make sure they actually *got* to the moon and back again.

Which was how, three days before Christmas 1968, NASA Astronauts Frank Borman, Jim Lovell and Bill Anders found themselves the very first men on their way there.

At the Apollo/Saturn V Centre to the west of Launch Complex 39, my fellow bus passengers and I waited patiently outside a set of double doors and watched a digital clock count down to zero.

This is what I really came to see, and I couldn't wait. I was a little confused though, because I had thought there was supposed to be a Saturn V moonrocket inside here somewhere and yet this building in front of me was only three or four storeys tall.

I was pretty sure the Saturn V was a little bit bigger than *that*.

When the clock finally reached zero, the doors opened to reveal a small, dark space. Three screens were hanging from the ceiling. A KSC staff member picked up a microphone and welcomed us, before a ten-minute film about how NASA got as far as *Apollo 8* began. By the time we got to Kennedy's rousing speech – 'We do these things...not because they are easy, but because they are *hard*' – I was already welling up.

All this stuff was just so goddamn *inspiring*. I couldn't help myself.

When the film ended – leaving us only hours from *Apollo 8*'s historic launch and the first real test of a Saturn V rocket – doors opened in front of us and we filed into a mock-up of the Firing Room, or Launch Control, as it looked in 1968. The workstations and displays are the real thing, and I got a kick out of the thought that NASA knew they had made a contribution to history so significant that it was required of them to preserve their clunky computer terminals for future generations to admire. Astronaut Jim Lovell appeared on screens above us and his buttery drawl filled the room. He was there to talk us through a re-enactment of *Apollo 8*'s launch.

Apollo 8 was going to make or break NASA's bid for a lunar landing. If everything went to plan, its crew would be the first to leave earth, traverse space and enter lunar orbit. If it didn't, three astronauts could be left forever circling the moon in a sarcophagus that America built and at Christmas time, no less. That's if NASA's slide rules, orbital mechanics and arithmetic were all sound and they managed to make it to the moon in the first place.

While Lovell talked about sitting in a tiny capsule fixed to the top of a Saturn V like the tip of the lead on a pencil, the screen showed hundreds of thousands of people gathered on the NASA Causeway and along the Indian River's banks to watch them fly to the moon on flames. As the Saturn V shook and shimmied and roared to life, it began to shed the blanket of ice that had formed on it while it waited, a hail of broken pieces that fell to the ground in showers, blurring the white edges of the rocket as it struggled to free itself from the launch pad's bonds. Flight Director Gene Kranz said it looked and sounded like it was alive.

Hold onto your hats, people.

At 363 feet tall, the Saturn V rocket had sixty feet on the Statue of Liberty and was longer than two Space Shuttles parked end to end. It weighed 6,000,000 pounds at launch and produced 7,500,000 pounds of thrust, or 160,000,000 horsepower. With the sole exception of a nuclear bomb, it produced the loudest noise ever made by the hand of man. It had nearly 6,000,000 moving parts but never failed, reliable enough to send *Apollo 8* to the moon on only its third ever flight. No one could be closer to it than three miles at launch; the Saturn had the explosive power of a million pounds of TNT and the shock waves alone would be enough to kill you. It burnt through twenty tons of fuel every second, or ten times more than Charles Lindbergh used to fly his solo-engine plane from New York to Paris only forty years earlier.

Per *second*.

After the simulated launch, complete with vibrations rattling the windows behind us, Lovell casually mentioned that he flew on two Saturns, the other being in April 1970 and on *Apollo 13*.

'But that's another story,' he quipped.

As his grandfatherly face faded out to black, yet another set of magic doors opened on the opposite side. Little Miss Eager Beaver here had been the first one in and now I was the first one out.

I was thinking, *Poor Jim Lovell. He never got to walk on the-*

[Prolonged pause with mouth hanging open.]

What the...?

I was twenty feet from the engine bell-end of a Saturn V, lying on its side and suspended on a frame above the floor. As people exited the Firing Room, conversation was stopping and footsteps were squeaking to a sudden halt on the linoleum floor.

It.

Was.

Enormous!

I walked around a bit, trying to take in the length, the sheer size, the circumference. Digital camera operators backed up against the windows behind us but still couldn't get more than a piece of it into a frame. About halfway down the exhibit hall people were sitting at the Moon Rock Cafe's tables, their eyes fixed on the monster above them while they absentmindedly shovelled pizza and fries into their mouths.

I was in the presence of an actual moonrocket. After landing five Apollo crews on the lunar surface, and with the Soviets well and truly beat, Americans turned their backs on the space program and NASA's once limitless funding all but dried up; the remaining Apollo missions were cancelled. While I was happy to see a real Saturn V at KSC, it should have been used to take men to the moon on *Apollos 18* or *19*. Instead, this Saturn V was helping visitors from all over the world understand the true meaning of the phrase 'mind-boggling.' Taking in its stats made my brain ache like it did when I tried to make sense of what was going on with *Lost*.

All day the dying embers of my Space Shuttle love affair had been threatening to go out forever and now seeing the Saturn V had just thrown ice-cold water over whatever was left. The Apollo program suddenly had what I'd once thought was exclusive to the Shuttle fleet: space sexiness. Yeah, the Orbiter was aerodynamic and sleek and cool and all, but just look at that Saturn V. They just strapped three guys to the top of this thing and *lit it*. They just set this monster *alight*!

Clearly I needed to calm down, so I walked purposefully to the other end of the hall and had a look at the Astronaut Van while simultaneously ignoring The Right Stuff gift shop on the other side. (Are those NASA logo *travel mugs*?) I lined up at the Lunar Theatre for a short presentation about Neil's small step and how it had enveloped the entire world in awe.

'For the first time,' the voice-over said, 'We were one people, with one history.'

I could cry right now, just thinking about it.

(I *am*!)

I decided to leave the ISS Centre for another day – there were sure to be plenty more of them over the next twelve months, now that I had my annual pass – and got on a bus that would take me back to the Visitor Complex.

En route, a video talked about how Merritt Island (the bit of the Cape that isn't KSC) is a nature reserve full of manatees, gators and birdlife, to name but a few. I was wondering how much more vicious the gators got when they've been all riled up by the vibrations of a Shuttle launch, when our driver stopped the bus to point out a bald eagle's nest in a tree on the roadside up head. Everyone else on the bus nearly broke their necks trying to get a good look but I was like, hello? I'm here to see space stuff, not *Animal Planet Live*.

I arrived right on time (i.e. thirty minutes early) for the next showing of *Magnificent Desolation: Walking on the Moon*, an IMAX movie presented by Tom Hanks, unofficial leader of the Armchair Astronauts. A space cadet since childhood, Hanks played Jim Lovell in the movie *Apollo 13* and went on to produce *From the Earth to the Moon*, a mini-series about the Apollo programme, which I had spent a glorious weekend watching from beginning to end.

I bought some M&Ms and a Coke from a lady who told me it was her dream to work in Disney World – I wanted to grab her by the shoulders and say, 'You work in KSC, woman. Get a grip!' – and took my seat in the theatre among sunburned British tourists, Type A American parents and the hyperactive offspring of both.

Seated in the row in front of me was a young couple fighting because Mummy had got herself a pair of 3D glasses and a pair for Daddy but neglected to get any for their young daughter who was sitting between them. After sulking in silence for a while, the woman turned to her husband and asked, 'Where is the Space Station?'

'I don't know what you mean.'

'Like, where is it exactly?'

'In space.'

'I *know* it's in *space*, honey. I'm not stupid.'

'Then I don't get what you're asking me.'

'I mean *where* is it. Like is it over France, or over China, or...'

I tried to turn off my ears, like I have to do in Epcot when I overhear blonde cheerleaders in shorts so short they should really only be worn under other shorts say things like, 'Well, the UK pavilion is like, totally Ireland as well. They're like, the *same*.' Either only stupid people come to Florida on vacation or there's some weird wrinkle in the space/time continuum that dumbs down everybody upon arrival. No doubt when Space Station Mummy got to Magic Kingdom, she'd be asking the Cast Members there at what time she should expect the three o'clock parade.

After a thoroughly enjoyable trip to the moon with Astronaut Hanks, I had a quick look in the Shuttle *Explorer*, a full-scale Orbiter replica whose interior KSC visitors can tour. It wasn't very...well, it wasn't very anything, really. The Boeing 747 that had brought me here from Ireland would completely dwarf it. Climbing the walkway, I passed displays highlighting the benefits of the Shuttle program for the rest of us back here on earth. Apparently experiments carried out onboard had resulted in safer roads, something about seat-belts, an environmental thingy...

It just all seemed a little desperate. The Shuttle never ventured further than 200 miles above the earth (or not very far, space-wise) and had cost – was still costing – billions and billions of taxpayer dollars. The more you looked around KSC, the more signs you saw that NASA was trying to win Space Shuttle fans.

I couldn't imagine the Saturn V pleading for support. It didn't have to. Just looking at it made you dizzy. Did I tell you they just strapped three guys to the top of that thing and *lit it*? They just set it *alight*! They just-

Okay.

Moving on.

My crossover to fully-fledged Apollo Gal now complete, I stopped at the Astronaut Memorial, a large black 'space mirror' that reflects the names of all the astronauts lost to the exploration of space. It includes the crews of *Apollo 1* (1967) and the Space Shuttles *Challenger* (1986) and *Columbia* (2003), and is maintained by the Astronaut Memorial Fund who collect a portion of the price of every special *Challenger/Columbia* license plate purchased in the State of Florida. Needless to say, one of them was on the back of my Mirage out in Wally Shirra.

The Space Shop, unsurprisingly, was two levels of everything I could have hoped for and more. I emerged after a heady forty-five minutes marvelling at my self-control. I had only bought a NASA baseball cap, an 'I Need My Space' keychain, a print of the moon and two books: *Light This Candle: The Life and Times of Alan Shepard* by Neal Thompson and *Apollo* by Charles Murray and Catherine Cox. Also in my possession: a list as long as the Saturn V of stuff I wanted to buy on my next visit.

Later on, six miles back along SR405, I couldn't quite figure out the Astronaut Hall of Fame. Admission is included with your KSC ticket and, in a display of Shuttle-like desperation, it stays open an hour later, hoping to snare you on the way home. The propaganda included with my KSC map claimed that the Hall of Fame was 'an interactive look at the life of an astronaut' and that it told the 'human story behind space travel...through the largest collection of personal astronaut memorabilia ever assembled.' There were also the 'stunning glass etchings' in the Hall of Heroes to look forward to. But as I pulled up outside a dirty white building surrounded by cracked pavement and stray weeds, I wondered if I had the right place.

Inside, the building had the noise of a public library and the liveliness of a morgue. The woman at reception directed me down a dark corridor towards a set of doors with automatic opening warnings.

Pushed against one wall were two garden benches. I'm not kidding – they were *literally* garden benches, the kind with varnished slats for a seat and a wrought iron frame. The TV monitors above the doors were switched off. After waiting for a few minutes and with nothing happening, my patience fizzled and I pushed open the doors.

Beyond was near total darkness. As my eyes

adjusted, I saw rows and rows of seats – *empty* seats – and a small projection screen at the top of the room. On the other side an identical set of double doors were just sliding closed. I took a seat, completely alone in the theatre at four in the afternoon.

A short film began to play, most of it completely out of focus. As best I could tell through the blur, it had something to do with Magellan, or maybe Columbus, with a little bit about Neil Armstrong thrown in at the end. A comparative study, maybe? I didn't really care. I was just after seeing the moon in all its IMAX 3-D glory and now I was trapped here, being subjected to someone's best efforts with Windows Movie Maker.

After five long minutes, the wretched thing ended and I was free to escape. On the other side of the doors was what I presumed was the promised 'collection of personal astronaut memorabilia' in glass display cases. There were some interesting items, including an original *Apollo 11* flight plan and a Western Union telegram from President Gerald Ford to the parents of *Apollo 1*'s Roger Chaffee, offering the President and First Lady's condolences.

The Hall of Heroes, although aptly named, was more disturbing than stunning. Tall blue podiums displayed eerie glass etchings of all the Hall of Famers, including Orlando's own John Young, one of NASA's most experienced astronauts and the namesake of one of the city's main thoroughfares, John Young Parkway. On learning of this honour, Young reportedly said dryly, 'Them boys shouldn't have done that. I ain't dead yet.'

I strode past the 'simulators' and 'hands-on activity' area – empty save for a couple of unsupervised kids running riot – and also managed to bypass my fourth space-themed gift shop of the afternoon.

More importantly, I made it all the way back to Orlando without getting pulled over. All in all, a successful day.

Of course, *Apollo 8* made it to the moon.

NASA Astronauts Borman, Lovell and Anders entered lunar orbit on Christmas Eve, 1968, after a near perfect trip of a quarter of a million miles. Their names would go down in history as the first among humankind to leave the bonds of earth behind them and bravely venture into the black and endless still of space.

Due to the angle at which *Apollo 8* approached, the moon was hidden from them until they were practically upon it. Then it swung out from the shadows, its grey and pockmarked surface illuminated by the bright light of the sun, filling the windows of their Command Module and touching the eyes of mankind for the very first time.

At 8.11pm, these three explorers began their ninth and penultimate orbit of the moon while back on earth, half a billion people tuned in for their live television broadcast.

The men began by sharing their impressions of the lunar surface, sixty-nine nautical miles below. They saw it as something both familiar and foreign, and they believed it offered them no invitation. The most surprising thing about travelling to the moon, they thought, was how small the earth seemed to be when they looked back at it – just a little thumbprint of a planet, suspended in a lonely vista. The astronauts were moved by the sight of their first 'earthrise' and Bill Anders took a picture of it to show the rest of us back home.

Before they signed off, the crew of *Apollo 8* said they had a special message for the people of earth. Anders flipped through the flight plan until he reached the extra insert at the back. Then he took a breath and began to read.

'In the beginning,' he said, 'God created the heaven and the earth. And the earth was without form, and void, and darkness was upon the face of the deep. And the spirit of God moved upon the face of the water. And God said, Let there be light...and there was light.'

Three days prior to this, Mission Control had advised *Apollo 8* that they were 'go to TLI'. *A Man on the Moon* author Andrew Chaikin calls this 'one of the most momentous directives ever given.' With this, man left the earth and made for the moon.

But that was just the beginning. After *Apollo 11* in July 1969, five more Apollo crews landed on the moon[2] and, on December 13th, 1972, Astronaut Gene Cernan was the last man to leave it. He and Harrison Schmitt had lived and worked on the lunar surface for three days and driven across its harsh terrain on a battery-powered car called the Lunar Rover.

More than thirty-five years later, Cernan can still say he was the last man on the moon.

The Apollo program was born of a race for supremacy and power. It was a task that united a nation and captivated the world, and it should have changed the course of our history forever. Even today, we should still be shaking our heads, wondering how such a thing could have been possible.

But just two missions after the first lunar landing, we had already changed the channel. Until an oxygen tank exploded onboard *Apollo 13's* Service Module, most people weren't even aware that anyone was up there – not one TV station carried the crew's live broadcast before the incident occurred. Of course, they were all replaying it afterwards.

Some people say the Apollo program never happened[3], while others say we cannot justify the

---

[2] *Apollo 13*'s lunar landing was aborted following an explosion en route.

[3] I don't talk to these people. The only thing more difficult than landing a man on the moon is pretending to land a man on the moon while the world watches and getting the 400,000 people who helped to keep their mouths shut for going on forty years. Give me a *break*.

expense of space exploration when problems closer to home need fixing. And to be honest, were I called upon to justify the Space Shuttle program, the construction of the ISS or – our next step – returning to the moon with an eye on Mars, I probably couldn't come up with anything better than I just think that we *should*.

Apollo is more than science or teamwork or exploration – it's inspiration. When *Apollo 17*'s Cernan talks to schoolchildren about his time in space, he tells them to take the word 'impossible' out of their vocabulary, because how can anything be impossible when he can say that he lived on the moon for three days and that he did it almost forty years ago?

We sent men to the moon at a time when the gap between such a triumph of technology and our everyday lives was just too great to span any real understanding of what was taking place. But the gap is far smaller today and we can now – we *should* now – turn back to that decade, when a piece of the future was transported to the past, and look at it anew.

The greatest lesson to be learned from travelling to the moon is one about ourselves here on earth and what we are capable of achieving. If you ever forget how great we all are, how magnificent and amazing and brilliant we are; if you ever doubt for a second just how much we can achieve, then walk outside some night and look up at the moon. Remind yourself that once, not long ago, one of us was up there.

And he was *driving around in a car*.

Back on *Apollo 8*, as both the crew's broadcast and Christmas Eve 1968 came to a close, Astronaut Borman said, 'Good night, good luck, a Merry Christmas, and God bless all of you, all of you on *the good earth*.'

Eleven
THE TOWN THAT DISNEY BUILT

One night back in the mid-nineties when I should have been doing my homework, I had happened to channel-surf onto the last few minutes of an intriguing documentary.

Just south of its world famous Orlando resort, the Walt Disney Company was breaking ground on its most ambitious project to date. Not another theme park, resort or attraction, but an entire town, built from scratch.

Since becoming Disney Chairman in 1984, Michael Eisner had succeeded in super-sizing Walt Disney World. By 1991, more than 20,000 hotel rooms had been added to the property along with yet another theme park, Disney-MGM Studios, and a collection of themed nightclubs called Pleasure Island. Construction of a fourth theme park, Disney's Animal Kingdom, was underway. Walt Disney World was now in a position to offer guests far more than world-class theme parks. It had become a place to sleep, dine, dance, golf, fish, sail or even learn to surf, albeit on a manmade wave at Typhoon Lagoon water park. Beyond its gates, an ugly rash of roach motels, greasy food outlets and fluorescent discount malls were no match for the manicured lawns and soothing visuals back inside them. Disney now, essentially, had the ultimate people-trap operated by a mouse; once they got you in, they did everything they could to keep you there.

But only a fraction of Disney's property had been developed and thoughts had turned now to the potential of the remainder. A Disney executive named Peter Rummell, head of a division called the Disney Development Company and therefore responsible for their real estate holdings, was tasked with evaluating this untouched Mouseland. His study concluded that even with everything Eisner and his Imagineers could dream of and more, the company's land south of Highway 192 was superfluous to their needs.

The land in question was 10,000 acres of marsh and swampland, home to swarms of mosquitoes and even the odd alligator; it was where Disney relocated the ones threatening to paddle around in its guest areas. Studies suggested that the best way to maximise the value of the land without adversely affecting the company's theme parks and resorts to the north would be to return to real estate in its most basic form: individual homes. Which is how, nearly a quarter of a century after Walt had revealed his plans for the Experimental Prototype Community of Tomorrow (EPCOT), Disney had finally come to build its own town.

But when plans were announced in 1991, it was obvious from the outset that Disney's Town of Celebration – a name suggested by Eisner's wife, Jane – would be the antithesis to EPCOT's futuristic skyscrapers and reflective glass. In fact the town would be far more like Main Street USA, with cookie-cutter cottages, front porches with rocking chairs, and picket fences – the very same school of Disney design that architectural historian Vincent Scully called 'unacceptably optimistic.'

However Celebration would at least be experimental. Based on the principles of New Urbanism, the town would strive to be a high-density, pedestrian-friendly place where residents could easily travel on foot from their homes to the downtown area. The lots would be small; the houses built only feet apart and with front porches set close to the street – all to encourage neighbourliness. Driveways and garages would be located to the rear and this, along with limited housing styles and a hefty 'Pattern Book' of strict covenants, would help maintain a pleasing and cohesive aesthetic. While a state of the art school and hi-tech 'health campus' would help lure in potential buyers to this picture-perfect enclave of small town America, the oversight of the Mouse would surely seal the deal.

Robert A. Stern was called upon to draw the master plans. At the time he was Dean of the Yale University School of Architecture and had recently designed Disney's Yacht and Beach Club Resorts. To preserve their autonomy, the Walt Disney Company de-annexed the area to neighbouring Osceola County. Otherwise, one day in the future, the colour of Cinderella's Castle might be decided on by the votes of Celebration residents.

The town broke ground in 1994. On November 18th, 1995 and before a single home was ready, more than 5,000 people gathered in Orlando to enter a lottery which would decide who among them would have the chance to bid on one of Celebration's first 350 homes, so much did demand exceed supply.

Today, the anniversary of this lottery draw is celebrated annually as Founders Day.

Back on the television, the shot changed from one of a construction site to a tidy billboard on the side of what was probably 192. Beneath a photo of a smiling little girl on a swing set, delicate lettering posed the question, 'Isn't this reason enough for Celebration?'

I, for one, thought it could well be.

Over the next ten years I kept an eye on the town's story.

Two journalists took up residence in Celebration for its first year and went on to write about their experiences;

I hungrily devoured both books and read them again and again. I frequented Celebration's official website, checking the rents on downtown apartments as if, at any moment, I might pack up everything and move to this small American town from a time I couldn't remember, happily growing old swinging on my porch, reading Hemingway in large print and waving to the neighbourhood children who, frankly, I didn't much care for.

For the US print media, Celebration was all their anti-corporate Christmases come together at once. By daring to build their own town, the Walt Disney Company had inadvertently handed the press hundreds of catchy headlines on a platter shaped like Mickey's head. The broadsheets screamed, 'DISNEY RULES A REAL KINGDOM,' 'IS THERE A MOUSE IN THE HOUSE?' and 'MICKEY MOUSE FOR MAYOR IN TOWN THAT DISNEY BUILT.'

Disney was ridiculed for extending itself into yet another facet of consumer life - now you could pour your Disney character breakfast cereal into your Disney bowl while sitting at a table from Disney's furniture line in your house that Disney built, wearing a Disney T-shirt and watching a Disney TV channel or talking on your Disney cell phone service, and then you could spend a day in the nearby Disney theme parks buying more Disney stuff with your Disney credit card. Mouse Haters warned that a hostile Disney take-over of the entire world could only be days away. When the founding residents proposed the building of a church in Celebration, the *Dallas Morning News* called it 'The First Church of Disney'. In the alarmist documentary *The Corporation*, the town is portrayed as a sinister experiment in subliminal brainwashing, populated by oblivious idiots only too happy to sign their souls away to the Mouse.

Much was made of the so-called 'rules' that residents agreed to abide by. These included no parking of boats, motor homes or trucks in front of homes; planting a certain percentage of their gardens with grass; showing only white window treatments to the street; and no visible TV aerials, satellite dishes or For Sale signs - in Celebration, there are only 'Homes Available'. These were hardly controversial regulations and wouldn't have warranted a second glance in any other master-planned community, but with a giant mouse-shaped shadow hanging over this one, every little detail came under scrutiny.

Within weeks of the first residents moving in, Celebration even had its very own urban legend. Somebody knew somebody who knew somebody who'd been strolling through downtown one morning when they'd encountered a young man walking a dog. Having stopped to admire the animal, they were shocked to learn from the young man that he was actually an on-duty Disney Cast Member, paid to walk around with the dog in an effort to make the place 'seem more real.'

To help get the town up and running, Celebration was initially advertised to Disney World guests and included on some WDW maps. Because Celebration's commercial district was fully leased and operational before the first residents arrived, the town needed a steady stream of tourists to keep these stores, boutiques and restaurants going until there were enough Celebrationites to support them. This guaranteed a regular influx of gawking visitors driving their rental cars through the streets at ten miles an hour, their heads out the windows. Early Celebration residents reportedly answered knocks on their doors, only to be met with complete strangers asking if they could come inside and look around. The public's perception of the place was confused at best and contemptuous at worse; many people thought it was just like Main Street USA, but with real people.

But Celebration *was* a real place, and it would soon have real problems to prove it.

It began with the homes themselves.

Celebrationites expected the same high standards, impeccable customer service and value for money they got when they visited the Disney theme parks - and why wouldn't they, with the same company responsible for both? Moreover, the price of a Disney World admission ticket wouldn't buy them a square foot of their new homes, and with big prices came even bigger expectations. But construction had struggled to match the pace of demand right from the outset and the contractors quickly drained the local area's supply of skilled tradesmen. The result was poorly erected homes riddled with confused wiring, pipes going nowhere and misread plans. ('TOWN BUILDING NO MICKEY MOUSE OPERATION' chuckled *The New York Times*.) Douglas Franz and Catherine Collins, authors of *Celebration, USA*, ended up with their neighbour's side porch on their property and hot water in their toilets.

But this inaugural crisis was quickly dwarfed by the second: the spectacular failure of Celebration's progressive school ('DISNEY'S MODEL SCHOOL: NO REASON TO CELEBRATE').

For many families, the town's biggest pull had been the promise of a technologically advanced centre for education. Incorporating cutting-edge teaching theory devised at Johns Hopkins and Harvard Universities, grades would mix in its special open classrooms or 'neighbourhoods' where students would be encouraged to study whatever topic happened to take their fancy. A suggested reading list for parents of potential students included titles like *Multiple Intelligences*, *Soar With Your Strengths* and *The Seven Habits of Highly Effective People*. There would be no traditional exams or report cards; students would be labelled 'Extending', 'Developing' or 'Not Yet'.

By the end of the first term, parents were worried that their offspring would be applying to the Ivy Leagues with an abstract finger painting and an essay on feelings.

In only its first year, Celebration's school lost sixteen of its twenty-one teachers and nearly all of its progressive ways.

Cracks were appearing in Disney's perfect town. To make matters worse for Disney, the whole sorry mess was right on their doorstep – literally. World Drive, the road to Magic Kingdom, had been specially extended to Celebration, forever tying the park to its third cousin in real estate. Less than two years after the first residents came to town, the Walt Disney Company began slowly distancing itself from the development.

One morning, Celebrationites awoke to discover that during the night, someone had scaled their (purely decorative) water tower and painted over the words 'Disney's Town of,' leaving Celebration on its own in more ways than one. Unsurprisingly, uproar ensued. The community felt like Disney was jumping off their sinking ship and leaving the stricken residents to their own devices. For its part, the company insisted that they were just anxious for Celebration to be thought of as a real place.

Once I discovered I'd be moving to Orlando for real, I began to look forward to getting a Celebration update.

Both of the journalist-turned-Celebration-resident accounts had been published in 1999 and after that, Celebration information had been difficult to come by. I wanted to know what had become of my favourite town in the meantime. At the beginning of my stay, pre-Mirage, I had no means of getting to the town itself, so I had to make do with pressing everyone around me for information on it.

Usually I was the only person who had ever even heard of Celebration, so I was a tad perturbed when I arrived in Orlando and found people casually throwing the town about in conversation - and not always in a good way. Some people spat the word out like a sour

Belgian chocolate, and you may as well have been accusing them of treason if you ever dared suggest they went anywhere near the place. Despite living in the world's largest theme park, Orlando residents could get quite indignant when you questioned the authenticity of their day-to-day experience.

Conversations about Celebration generally went one of three ways. The populist stance seemed to be that it was unjustifiably expensive to shop or eat there. Then there were those who disapproved on principle - Celebration-Haters who spewed angry tirades about it being Phase II of Disney's dastardly plan for world domination. But the vast majority didn't have the first clue what Celebration was. This became clear to me when I asked someone what 'Reunion' was; one of agents had recently gone to work there. 'Oh, it's this new golf resort where you can, like, stay in a hotel, or you can buy a house there and rent it out. It's a Celebration kind of thing,' was the explanation.

But by far my most disturbing discovery was the rumoured New Celebration: a sub-community of British ex-pats for whom the favourable exchange rate not only substantially increased their real estate buying power, but also kicked them up a couple of social classes as well. Back home in gloomy England, they spent Saturdays watching football matches in their boxy semi-Ds but here in Florida, they spent Saturdays watching soccer games on plasma televisions in the great rooms of their multi-million dollar McMansions. When these *nouveau riche* told people they lived in Celebration what they really meant was that they were rich enough to live there. I had the unfortunate experience of meeting one of these New Celebrationites in Raglan Road, the Irish bar and restaurant at Downtown Disney. I was sitting at the bar with a friend when this rather large individual next to me struck up a conversation.

His name was Andy and he sounded like he had just walked off the set of *Eastenders*. Perched on a bar stool, his sizeable girth reached almost to his knees and his bulbous face was pink with sunburn. Andy was in Raglan Road that night trying to poach patrons for the British sports bar he had just opened in Celebration, the same venture that had earned him his US visa.

In my head, Celebration was the epitome of saccharine suburbia: porch swings, block parties and American flags. Even if Mickey was the mayor and the town a corporate invention, it was still an idyllic place to escape from the noise of modern life. I thought the people who moved there did so to return themselves and their families to a simpler time, one that usually predated them. They were searching for the perfect place to call home.

So where did Andy and his brash British bar fit in?

We chatted with him and his girlfriend for some time, and I laughed politely as they regaled us with the scandalous behaviour Celebration's expat community had been getting up to - mainly cheating on spouses with the neighbours' au pairs, apparently. But my mind was elsewhere. Had Celebration become as theatrical as the company who'd built it? Was it like another famous picture-perfect piece of suburbia, where everything looked nice on the outside, but was dramatically coming apart from within? Maybe *Desperate Housewives* and the town of Celebration shared more than a street named after wisteria.

All my Celebration information was about five years out of date and seemed to bear no resemblance to the town I was hearing about now. What about the people who had travelled from all over the world to put their name in the Founders Day lottery, chasing an ideal place to raise their family? What about the Disneyphiles, the Mouse fanatics who jumped at the chance to live so close to the Castle, and in a town built on the same innocent happiness as Magic Kingdom? Where were they?

I needed to get to Celebration. I wanted to see for myself what the town had become.

Following my success in driving the sixty miles to Kennedy Space Centre, I decided the time was right to brave I-4 and finally experience Celebration. Again, I elected to do this on my own, without anyone complaining in my ear about high prices and fakery. I was hoping that if I got beyond the evenly spaced palms and faux dormer windows, I would find some pixie dust still lingering in the air.

It was one of those beautiful breezy days that made you think you could feasibly live in Florida forever. When I started out around ten in the morning, traffic on I-4 was light and calm, but I was still relieved to reach Celebration's exit, marked by an electricity pylon in the shape of Mickey's silhouette. Turning right opposite Celebration Health, I met my first row of Celebration homes, which reminded me a little bit of the Sylvanian Families toy line I had played with as a child.

I found it difficult to equate the view out the windscreen with the town I had dreamed of living in for so long. The houses looked pretty much as I imagined they would – I had seen countless photos of them, after all – but something just wasn't quite right with the place. I hadn't expected it to feel so...well, *real*.

To me, Celebration was just like *The Truman Show's* fictional setting of Seahaven, whose inhabitants skipped merrily along, enraptured with the delight of living in a clapboard paradise. *The Truman Show*, incidentally, had been filmed in another Floridian New Urbanist development called Seaside. Celebration was a place where strangers greeted each other warmly on the street; where the sun always shone and where, if you wanted to, you could completely forget there was any other kind of world outside its walls.

I was all for escapism, even if it came from a business plan.

After parking the car – a bit sideways, but still inside the lines – I frowned at the scarcity of spaces in the lot hidden behind one of downtown's apartment buildings.

Apparently they hadn't quite got the hang of New Urbanism just yet. But then, how could they? They did live in Orlando after all, where I could personally testify that life without a car was no life at all. I could see that some residents were using electronic carts to get around the town, but I still considered that a contravention. True New Urbanites would be using their feet.

Strolling down the imaginatively named Front Street in front of the lake, I passed a construction site, a couple of skateboarding teenagers and – was that a *Starbucks*? My Celebration books told of how Disney had gone to great lengths, somewhat ironically, to keep chain stores out of downtown, renting instead to carefully chosen quirky stores and boutiques. Since then, the Green Apron Army had evidently elbowed their way in.

Celebration's downtown has it arms around the manmade Celebration Lake with the rest of the town spread out behind it. If it wasn't for Osceola County prohibiting the repetition of street names, Celebration's Market Street would have been Main Street, and the Mouse Haters would have one more thing to poke fun at. I went as far as the small plaza at the opposite end and the vaguely nautical post office designed by Michael Graves, the architect of Walt Disney World's Swan and Dolphin Hotels. I window-shopped at some of the stores and wondered idly if the friendly smiles of passers-by were proof that they were real, live Celebration residents, or just visitors like me trying not to stand out.

I returned to the prettiest part of Celebration: Front Street, on the lake's edge. Rocking chairs and parasols invite those with the time to sit down and relax, and a fountain – similar to the one at Downtown Disney's Marketplace – spurts columns of water high into the air, encouraging children to soak their clothes and run around on wet cement. Signs remind everyone that it is against Florida law to feed the alligators.

What *did* Disney do with all those gators?

The most distinctive feature on Front Street is the

AMC movie theatre designed by Cesar Pelli, its twin white spires looking like 'space age' did in the Fifties. Just like Epcot, and Tomorrowland at Magic Kingdom, Disney's future is the tomorrow of yesterday. Juxtaposed with housing styles that ranged from Colonial to Victorian to Greek Revival, Celebration's downtown prompted urban theorist Kevin Lynch to ask, 'What time *is* this place?' But then you had to wonder how many urban theorists had decided to buy houses in the town that Disney built.

Next to the theatre is something far more interesting: Reading Trout Books. It offers only the scantest collection of titles but has huge leather armchairs that practically order you to sit in them, and it stocks the daily newspapers. Just inside the door are several shelves of Disney titles and hardcover editions of my Celebration books. I sat for a while and leafed through *Celebration: The Story of a Town* by Michael Lassell. This weighty coffee table volume celebrates, if you'll forgive the pun, the town's place in history as an experiment in social engineering, an achievement often overcast by a gigantic Mickey-shaped shadow. The bookstore's proprietor was keeping track of her out-of-town visitors on a globe by the register but, alas, some other Irish person had been there before me and their pin was taking up our entire country.

I decided to leave Celebration via 192, a long and ugly stretch of Strip Mall USA, and the first place to suffer an explosion of secondary retailers, all hoping to cash in on their new Disney neighbour. These days, it's the other way around.

Capitalising on Celebration's infamy, the Water Tower – another imaginative name, it being the site of the actual Celebration water tower – is a modern shopping mall only an aluminium picket fence away from 192. Despite the matching white buildings, there's no disguising that this is the very thing Celebration and its New Urbanism was supposed to avoid: a local grocery store you have to drive to. All the usual suspects are here, including a couple of drive-thru fast food restaurants, a SunTrust branch, a coffee shop and a Gooding's, set against a backdrop of speeding traffic roaring past only feet away.

Evidently this piece of prime real estate was too good an opportunity to pass up, even if it did fly in the face of everything the town reportedly stood for. But then Disney didn't get where they are today by turning a blind eye to the bottom line.

America had convinced me that she was not a land of opportunity, as the rest of the world had been led to believe, but one of broken dreams, empty promises, credit card debt and car payments. Orlando seemed to be a city without a centre, serving only as a slave to its rodent custodian. And now even Celebration was beginning to look like a Cinderella's Castle built of sand. It was going to break my heart to have to relegate a town that had lived so vividly in my dreams to those sad ranks.

I had no interest in talking to the *nouveaux riches* blow-ins who had seemingly ascended to the top of Celebration society, even though I still hoped there was no such thing as 'Celebration society' beyond the one that these New Celebrationites imagined in their heads. What I wanted to know was what had become of the characters in my Celebration books - the pioneers who had travelled to the original lottery, who had sacrificed their old lives to move to the town that Disney built, and whose fortunes I'd followed as they tried to steer their way through the town's difficult birth. Many people who bought one of the original 350 homes had had to beg, borrow and steal to come up with the money; behind the door of many a newly-built Celebration home were empty or sparse rooms because mortgage payments had left almost nothing for new furniture.

Where were these people, and what did they think of what the town had become?

Then one day I discovered, quite unexpectedly, that there had been a Celebration founder under my nose the entire time.

One slow afternoon at the Duck desk I got chatting to Maggie, one of the Disney Cruise Line representatives with whom we shared the counter. I nearly collapsed in a heap on the floor when she told me that she and her husband had entered the original Founders Day lottery, back in 1995. She might as well have told me that she was sitting on the moon in a deckchair when Neil Armstrong arrived.

Maggie was a soft-spoken yet dedicated Disneyphile. Her and her husband had visited all five Disney parks around the world (Florida, California, Paris, Hong Kong and Tokyo), vacationed on the Disney Cruise Line and travelled from their home in Philadelphia to Disney World whenever they had a chance. As soon as they heard that Disney was building a town, they packed up everything and moved down south for good.

Circumspect about the problems the town had faced, Maggie was reluctant to condemn Disney for Celebration's problems. This reluctance didn't stem from any illogical corporate loyalty or naiveté - in fact, Maggie was just realistic. As much as she believed in the magic of Disney, she never for a second thought that moving to Celebration would be a walk in a Disney theme park.

Maggie's husband had secured a position as a Disney shuttle bus driver, and Maggie herself had worked in the Celebration Store, a short-lived gift shop that sold various mugs, shirts and other items emblazoned with Celebration's logo. She did admit that there'd been 'one or two' issues with their house, but maintained they'd been quickly resolved by the construction company. And 'the thing with the school' had little impact on their family because both her children were high school seniors the year they moved in. Her only gripe was the closure of Market Street's grocery store and its relocation to the Water Tower shopping complex.

She was surprised to learn that books had been written about her town and I was surprised to learn that she had absolutely no interest in reading them.

For Maggie and her family, the Celebration they lived in today was very different from the one that had drawn them to Florida originally. For many years now, the Mouse had been conspicuously absent. Disney couldn't vet Celebration residents like they could their Cast Members, so regardless of what they thought of Celebration or how they treated it, anyone could live there. But if the town was really going to work, if it was ever going to hold its original vision in clear focus, then it would take a certain kind of community.

One that, at the very least, revered neighbourliness and savoured life's simpler pleasures, and not one that insisted on driving their Ferrari through downtown at high speed, the tires screeching, *Look at me! I live in Celebration! I have money!*

I tried to imagine what it must have felt like to see a dream you wished for your family slip away in circumstances beyond your control, leaving you with little other than a hefty mortgage to show for it, but Maggie didn't harbour any regrets. Celebration was still a wonderful place to live – it was beautiful and quiet, and there was a great sense of community amongst the majority of its residents. After their kids had left for college, Maggie and her husband sold their three-bedroom house and downsized to an apartment but they chose to stay in Celebration. Wishing on a star hadn't quite worked out but, in their eyes, both Disney and their family had emerged unscathed and maybe even better off for it.

I visited Celebration again the day after I talked to

Maggie.

While waiting for my breakfast at the Market Street Café – a diner with a subtle retro theme, a great view of the lake and a kick-ass cafe latte – I browsed the latest edition of *Celebration News*. On its pages were local kids done good, photos from some recent festival and a gentle reminder that only one small political yard sign was allowed per lawn, and that it must disappear no later than two days after the election. A large property section seemed to imply that the entire town was up for sale.

Afterwards I stopped by the lake, and settled into a rocking chair to admire the view. On a bench nearby was a group of four Japanese tourists studying a pamphlet for the Celebration Hotel; an elderly woman walked past with a little poodle; a young couple pressed their laptops together at a table outside Starbucks.

It's impossible to forget that not very far from here, a slice of the Orlando I loved to hate was waiting patiently for me to return. In less than five minutes, I would be back on 192 and driving past decrepit motels that reminded me of horror movies, the weird fruit store shaped like a giant orange and that patronising billboard that has me cursing it every time (*'The real Supreme Court meets up here'* – God). And undoubtedly, somewhere in the picturesque town behind me, there were unpaid bills and loveless marriages, a problem child, or a living room with no furniture because, beautiful as it was, the town behind me was still a *real* town.

But you couldn't see any of that from where I was sitting at that moment. That doesn't mean that Celebration keeps real life away, but it can provide temporary sanctuary from the uglier bits of it. Maybe I should have been concerned with the evils of Disney, or sales brochures that promised not just a new home but a new life, or maybe I should have been angry about the lie that the fake dormer windows represented, but I didn't think I could convince myself to care. Happiness – even fleeting moments of it – is hard to come by, and in my search for it I'd realised that the only manufactured happiness I was against is the one you get from ingesting pharmaceuticals.

I didn't worry about whether or not I was being brainwashed while I watched Wishes; I wouldn't start worrying about it while I walked around Celebration.

And besides, none of that would change how I felt right then, as I sat there by the edge of the lake. Sometimes, in Celebration, if you stay really, really still, you can detect the faint scent of pixie dust lingering in the air.

Twelve
ADVENTURES IN HUMIDITY

Summer was coming.

Central Floridians dreaded July and August, when the average daily temperature would exceed those on the surface of the sun, according to my Florida resident friends. But then again, these were the same people who had promised that it would get cold in January.

'You didn't think it got cold?' one of my colleagues said, incredulous. 'What are you talking about? I had to wear a sweater at night for *a whole week!*'

The summer season would also bring with it an influx of British and Irish holidaymakers and herds of South American schoolchildren on school tours. Florida resident pass holders would be locked out of Walt Disney World's parks and Orlando would slow to a crawl as thousands of rental cars infiltrated the morning commute. For the next eight weeks, you'd be constantly reminded that you had chosen to live in the world's most popular tourist destination, and the only thing to do was hunker down inside your air-conditioned apartment and wait for it all to pass.

But something else was coming too: my brother John, on a two-week visit. In the midst of this stifling heat and suffocating humidity, he and I were going to experience Orlando the way it was meant to be – as tourists – and I was going to get to be the Big Sister I'd always wanted to have, hosting my little brother for the most hectic fourteen days of my entire Florida experience.

Ready. Set. *Go.*

Day 1: Arrival

He's here!

To avail of a cheaper fare, John had flown from Cork to Orlando via Amsterdam or, in other words, started his journey by flying for two and a half hours in the wrong direction. He arrived at the Duck – I was working – at around eight in the evening, full of stories of over-friendly middle-aged American women he'd got chatting to (or been attacked by) on the airport shuttle en route to the hotel.

I showed him briefly around the hotel, introduced him to the Mirage, and after a couple of drinks at Raglan Road, we called it a night. John had had a long, arduous day of traveling, and we had a busy fortnight ahead of us.

Day 2: The Space Coast

Needless to say, our first activity was Kennedy Space Centre.

Officially, my reasoning for this was because it would be less tiring for jet-lagged John than a full day at a Disney park, but really it was because I couldn't wait a moment longer to try out the brand new Shuttle Launch Experience, KSC's first thrill ride.

Designed by astronauts, this simulator was supposed to be an authentic recreation of an actual Shuttle launch and had opened to great fanfare – and some space-celebrity riders, including Orlando-born

Astronaut John Young – only a few weeks earlier. It was housed in a new building off the Visitor Complex main plaza, near the Space Shuttle *Explorer*.

I should point out that I don't do thrill rides. I hate rollercoasters; I can't understand why anyone would want to pay money for the experience of feeling that their death by blunt force trauma is imminent. Magic Kingdom's Thunder Mountain is about as extreme as it gets for me and I only do that to appease the people I go to the parks with. (There was one time I really did enjoy my ride on Thunder Mountain – Andrea and I rode it at night in the front row of the first car while a biblical thunderstorm unleashed hell directly above us. Now *that* was fun.)

Ted had already ridden the Shuttle Launch Experience and I had pressed him for details, i.e. how likely was I to suffer a bout of motion sickness and upchuck all over the flight deck? He assured me that it fine, the worst of it was 'a bit of shaking.' But even if he'd told me it was Epcot's Mission Space meets Magic Kingdom's Space Mountain meets freebasing off Mount Everest than I still would have done it, because it was the closest I was ever going to get to the real thing.

After securing our bags, our cameras and fetching KSC ponchos (it was raining, okay?), we filed up the walkway and into our pre-flight training session, led by NASA Astronaut (and future NASA Administrator) Charlie Bolden. Then it was into another holding room where we were given yet more safety instructions – including doomsday warnings about 'falling debris' – before being directed to our seats on a pretty good mock-up of a Shuttle's flight deck. Once strapped in, the simulator pivoted until we were lying on our backs, just as real Shuttle astronauts would be as they counted down to launch.

Then we had the crap shaken out of us.

When the neck-snapping vibrations – or 'launch', apparently – stopped and we were 'in space', we were pushed back up into sitting position and then forward a bit again. This made us slide out of our chairs and up against the restraints – hanging, but not uncomfortably. A truly ingenious way to manipulate gravity enough to make us feel like there wasn't any; we were weightless.

As we marvelled at that, the cargo bay doors above us – above us for the purposes of this ride, anyway – opened to reveal a stunning view of the earth from earth orbit, surrounded by dots of shining stars. Space, for all intents and purposes. It was beautiful, but it made me sad – I wanted to go do it for real.

After we left KSC mid-afternoon, I drove us to Cocoa Beach even though it wasn't really a day for it, just so John could go home and say he'd seen the Atlantic from the other shore.

I wasn't quite sure of the way and ended up on some rural back roads, so it turned out John was able to say he'd seen a few trailer parks as well.

Day 3: Disney Day I

Our tight schedule called for us to do two parks on Saturday, and so after a delicious breakfast of coffee and chocolate croissants at the Boardwalk Bakery, we hit Disney-MGM Studios and Epcot.

John loved Soarin' as much as I did and I got to watch Illumi-NATIONS from inside Epcot for the very first time.

Day 4: Disney Day II

We spent our fourth day touring Magic Kingdom.

Leaving the park before Wishes was against everything I stood for so to ensure we hadn't exhausted ourselves by closing time, we delayed going in until noon and instead enjoyed Sunday brunch at the Market Street

Cafe in Celebration.

Later we got our photo taken with the Big Mouse himself and I got all of Wishes on video, AKA Prozac on DVD.

Day 5: Disney Day III

I'd never been to Animal Kingdom, Disney World's newest park, but, it being evidently all about animals, I wasn't exactly sleepless with excitement.

Walking in first thing Monday morning, I felt a bit claustrophobic. Unlike the other Disney parks, AK was filled with miniature forests of tropical palms and other plantation, blocking your view every which way. This was in stark contrast to say, Magic Kingdom or Epcot, where you could see straight across the park.

But it proved to be a lot more fun, overall, than I was expecting, especially the Kilimanjaro Safari, an open-sided truck ride through 110 acres of manmade African savannah and the most popular attraction in the park. It seemed pretty real, at least compared to what I've seen on TV - the only thing missing was a *National Geographic* camera crew.

At one point in the day we were crossing a bridge when we spotted Minnie, dressed appropriately in khakis, on a boat with her Disney handlers on the river below. The children on the bridge starting waving and before I knew what I was doing, I started waving too, getting a little thrill when Minnie – or rather, the diminutive eighteen-year-old girl inside the Minnie costume – started enthusiastically waving back.

What was Disney *doing* to me?

Day 6: Sea World

In the larger scheme of Orlando attractions, Sea World is

a bit of a snooze fest - the made-for-TV movie to Disney's Best Picture - except when it comes to two things that only Sea World has: Shamu and free beer.

Shamu Rocks, the trained killer whale extravaganza that takes place in the enormous Shamu Stadium, was one of the best experiences of my entire eighteen-month stay in Florida. Darkness had fallen and the deep waters of the enormous tank in the stadium's centre were lit from underneath. The capacity crowd cheered and danced to the pre-show music, and then Sea World's team of trainers and the stars of the show - Shamu the XIV, or however many, his wife and children - performed literally *unbelievable* stunts to rock music.

But while I'd choose Disney any day, there is one thing you can do in Sea World - for *free* - that isn't even allowed in Magic Kingdom, and that's drink beer. The park belongs to Anheuser-Busch, who produce, among other alcoholic beverages, Budweiser. As long as you are over twenty-one and have the ID to prove it, you can have free beer. And not just once, but all the livelong day.

My Sea World 'Fun Card' ticket, which would allow me to return as many days as I liked at no extra charge until the end of the year, was going to pay for itself.

Day 7: Gatorland

I would have never gone to Gatorland if it wasn't for John's childhood gator obsession and the cheap tickets (we got in for less than thirty dollars, or one third of a Disney ticket) but if I hadn't gone, it would have been a terrible shame.

Family-run and family-friendly, Gatorland proved to be a great day out. Sure, there were plenty of gators to look at - and a guy willing to stick his head between their jaws for us to look at as well - but there were also beautiful forests to walk through, a new water adventure area for kids (and adults, looking to cool off in the summer heat) and all in all, a really nice place to spend an afternoon.

Day 8: My Birthday

On Thursday, I turned twenty-one for the fifth year in a row.

We began the morning with shopping and Starbucks at Orlando's beautiful Mall at Millennia, and then, after I'd finished work, we celebrated the occasion at Universal's answer to Downtown Disney, City Walk.

The less said about what happened there the better but I will say this: it would have been nice to get through life without my little brother ever seeing me projectile vomit.

I blame the Hurricanes.

Days 9, 10 & 11: Washington D.C.

When I found out my brother was coming to visit, I booked flights to and accommodation in Washington D.C. on a whim; Andrea had never been and I wanted John to see as much as possible on his short trip to the States. As it turned out, our gang of three was able to meet up with my cousin David, who was living in Towson, Maryland, and his girlfriend Clíona, visiting from Ireland, and we had a truly fantastic weekend.

Thoroughly hungover, the trip seemed like it was off to a bad start when I realised I'd left our boarding passes in work the night before. However it all worked out and, skipping over a long story, we not only made it to the airport in time and with our boarding passes, but we were driven there in a stretch limousine.

D.C. was a delight for a *West Wing* fanatic like me. We managed a whistle-stop tour of all its famous sights: the Capitol Building (Andrea generously arranged a tour for us through her Congressman), the Lincoln Memorial, the Jefferson Memorial, the Roosevelt Memorial, the Washington Monument, the White House, the Library of Congress, the US Supreme Court and, last but not least, *The Exorcist* steps off Prospect Avenue in Georgetown.

Day 12: Downtown Disney

With only a couple of days of John's visit left, it was time to tie up some loose ends.

We toured the grounds of the Duck and Tuna, did a bit of last minute shopping and then finally hit Downtown Disney for a walk around the Virgin Megastore and a movie in the AMC.

(*Die Hard*, in case you're wondering. I had to let him choose.)

Day 13: Universal Studios

Then suddenly John had only one full day left in Orlando.

We would spend it in Universal's Orlando Resort, a sprawling complex just off I-4 with two theme parks – Universal Studios and Islands of Adventure – and City Walk, a pristine shopping and dining area spread around the banks of a picturesque lake between the entrances to the other two. I had never been before and we were both quite looking forward to it.

We began our day by getting our photo taken in front of Universal's famous rotating globe and then headed into Universal Studios.

Everyone in Orlando will tell you that while Disney is magical, Universal is *fun*, and I soon saw what they meant. After the amazing *Terminator 3-D*, we practically ran to the park's recreation of Amity, the fictional town in *Jaws* that was a wee bit of a killer shark magnet, where

I was literally the only person in the entire boat who managed to get soaked. Next up was *Earthquake*, a staple of Universal Studios in California, recreated here; a clip of it always seemed to end up on holiday programs presented by Judith Chambers. It's the ride where you're sitting on a subway train when the ground shakes, the street above sinks, a tanker comes crashing towards you and there's lots and lots of fire and water. Terrifying fun for all the family.

In the late afternoon, we made our way through City Walk to Islands of Adventure, a park consisting solely of rides that shoot you up or down or around a track at death-defying speeds, with your arms or legs or head dangling, throwing in sudden stops or loops or corkscrews or reversals every now and then just to mix it up. The park's map was filled with attractions with names like Doctor Doom's Fear Fall, Poseidon's Fury and Duelling Dragons – that last one being two rollercoasters that ran straight at each other as if about to collide only to swing away in opposite directions at the very, very last second, or about three seconds after I'd have had a heart attack. So why were John and I, self-confessed coaster phobics, even here?

Two words: *Jurassic Park*.

In the summer of 1993 the best movie ever made had been released, and eleven-year-old me had gone to the cinema to see it with nine-year-old John. CGI Dino Mania had gripped the world and Cork was no exception – the queue for tickets was all the way down the street and around the corner.

This would be my second time seeing JP. A week earlier I had gone to see it with my cousin Aisling, the same Aisling who I'd meet up with thirteen years later in Orlando, but we had watched most of it through our fingers, absolutely terrified. I was hoping to see a few more scenes this time round.

I had laboriously read as much of the book as I could (I still have that movie tie-in paperback, although due to annual re-readings it's now just about held together with tape), and everything that summer seemed to have the black, red and yellow *Jurassic Park* logo on it (I had the binder, pencil case and notebook). In special issues of *Smash Hits* magazine, I had read all about Mr. Spielberg's dinosaurs and how they had been created, and I was glued to any behind the scenes documentaries shown on TV. As I got older I was finally able to understand the bits of the novel thick with genetics and chaos theory, and I progressed to more age-appropriate merchandise, like a special-edition DVD and John Williams' original score.

When I discovered a *Jurassic Park* ride at Universal I knew that no matter what, I had to brave it.

And it was more than a ride; it was a recreation of Jurassic Park itself. You walked through the same foreboding gates, you passed the same logoed Ford Explorers, and you could have your lunch - or buy plastic dinos - in the same Visitors' Centre that was left to the velociprators and their T-Rex friend in the final scenes of the movie.

Then there was the Jurassic Park River Adventure: ninety-five percent a gentle boat ride through JP's dinosaur enclosures, and five percent a bit of a drop. It we didn't do the drop we couldn't do the river ride before it, so we threw caution to the wind and joined the queue.

What we didn't know at the time was that the JP River Ride boasted the biggest drop of any thrill ride in *the entire world*, a long eighty feet from top to bottom.

You can see where this is going.

After a pleasant trip along the river – and through some excellently recreated scenes from *Jurassic Park* – our 'boat' started climbing up through what looked like the ducts and vents of a factory, or the insides of a huge machine. Whatever it was, it did a very good job of disguising how high up we were climbing – the incline wasn't very steep and our progress was slow. At the top, a pair of scary dinosaur jaws snapped out at us from a dark corner and then-

Down - *straight* down.

And fast.

I may have had a little heart attack.

Just as we were about to go over the edge, my survival instincts kicked in and I gripped with both hands the foam-covered bar that ran across the back of the row of seats in front of me. Tightly. I knew I wasn't going to go anywhere (I *hoped* I wasn't) but I liked the reassurance of holding on. But as our trajectory switched from up to down, the angle and speed at which we fell was so great that I couldn't hold on to the bar without feeling like I was coming out of my seat and over it; all I could do was place my palms flat on the foam and push back like I would do against the dashboard of a car to brace myself against a head-on collision.

All I could hear were screams.

My own, everyone else's.

It took merely seconds for us to crash into the water below but it felt like a full minute or more of freefall. The force of getting back down to the ground from eighty feet straight up left me feeling like I'd had a blow-dry and a facelift. My pulse was coming out through my neck.

Jelly-legged, our faces white and slackened, staring at the people lined up to get on as if they were dangerously insane, John and I looked at each other.

Never, *ever* again.

Day 14: Homeward Bound

The next morning, I brought John and his suitcase full of purchases to Orlando International Airport. It had been a fantastic fortnight, but now I needed to sleep – for a few days, maybe even a week.

Back at my apartment, I cranked up the A/C, lay on my bed with a book, and then stayed that way for the rest of the summer.

Thirteen
COFFEE HAS TWO 'f's

After a summer of too few easy-to-please business travellers and too many impossible-to-please holidaymakers, by the time my one-year Orlando anniversary rolled around I found myself suffering from Front Desk Agent Burn Out.

I loved working Front Desk, for the most part. You could always count on meeting nice people and I genuinely enjoyed being able to make a good stay great if I could. I even got a self-affirming sense of achievement whenever I managed to resolve some issue or problem, especially if a resolution had seemed unlikely at the outset. But the desk wasn't without its drawbacks too, the biggest one being that eventually, every check-in became the same. You were constantly repeating the same questions, information and directions, and you'd pretty much learned everything you or your guests were ever going to need to know about shuttle buses, opening hours, ways to get to the pool and the best place to watch the Epcot fireworks if you weren't in the park.

I was getting kind of bored.

Coincidentally, an infamous incident involving a staff barbecue, a roll of my eyes and an alleged 'negative attitude' had the Front Office Manager's evil yet attractive eyes looking in my direction. He clearly had his favourites and I, for whatever reason, wasn't one of them. He wanted to get rid of me or, in Corporate America-speak, strategically redistribute my core competencies to a department where they'd prove impactful in a more workable time frame.

And he did.

He banished me to Housekeeping.

I didn't figure this out right away though. The banishment bit, I mean.

When he called me into his lair and told me that he was trying to get me promoted to the position of Housekeeping Inspector, all I could think about was the fact that I wouldn't have to wear pantyhose or work at night anymore.

And did you say *promoted*?

I didn't think about how in reality it meant a paltry seventy-five cents more an hour, or how the people I'd be supervising would passionately hate me, or how the position was generally regarded throughout the hotel as being the very worse one. Everyone recognised the Inspector Team: the women running – literally *running* – around the hotel with their radios beeping and their brows shiny with sweat, while their subordinates, the Room Attendants, openly laughed at them, ignored everything they said and tore them to shreds behind their backs.

Or sometimes, in front of their faces.

Not to mention the fact that I was just not cut out to be in housekeeping. My mother had spent my childhood (and my adolescence, and some of my adulthood) despairing over the state of my bedroom. I understood nothing about the phrase 'putting things back where they belong' and when clothes came off, they tended to stay where they fell. And was there anything more pointless than making a bed only to mess it up again later that same day?

I, like, totally doubt it.

Now I was going to be responsible for making sure a team of Room Attendants cleaned 150 rooms to an acceptable standard every single day. Not only was I going to have to learn how to make the beds up with the dizzying array of sheets, pillows, and decorative cushions the hotel deemed necessary for the job, but I was going to have to fold these sheets into hospital corners.

Other than being a midwife (I don't do childbirth – I can't even watch people in labour on *Friends*) or a lifeguard (I don't do water deeper than I am tall), this was the most unsuitable job I could possibly have.

In more bad news, I was going to be a Housekeeping Inspector at the Tuna side of the hotel. This meant I'd be leaving behind the quieter, family-like environment of the Duck for the monstrous sprawl of the Tuna wing, all panic and energy, and with more than 1,500 guest rooms.

And I hated the Tuna's cafeteria to boot: the food wasn't as good as it was in the Duck, and going in there reminded me of those scenes from US teen movies where some social outcast stands with tray in hand at the top of the school cafeteria, looking for a spot to sit somewhere amidst the gangs and cliques.

My promotion didn't exactly generate a slew of congratulatory high-fives from my colleagues and friends. Instead, they could only offer their sympathy and commiserations. But I needed to get out of Front Desk, I told them. I needed a challenge, a change of scenery; of pace. They weren't convinced but in fairness to them, they played along.

It was like the time I dyed my hair red when I was thirteen and my friend, solicited for a reaction, said, 'You like it like that, do you?'

Meanwhile my last day on the desk was an emotional one - well, this is *me* we're talking about – with cake and balloons and a lot of reminiscing. After all,

Andrea and I – now best buds and the apartment-sharing equivalent of soul mates – had nearly worked the same shift every day for the past ten months.

Later I would see the benefits of leaving Front Desk before I left Orlando. If the two had occurred at the same time, I would've been in bits.

Almost a year to the day after I arrived in Florida I reported to the Tuna Housekeeping Department for duty.

I was sent to find my new direct line manager who, I was told, was at the Room Attendants' (RAs) pre-shift meeting. This was where 'the ladies' - as the RAs were called, even though some of them were men - were assigned rooms to clean and given the keys to them before being sent upstairs onto the guest floors.

I walked into a room of about forty RAs, all dressed in their blue and white uniforms, standing around a table where Housekeeping management presided over room lists and boxes of Master Keys, and it seemed like every single one of them was screaming, shouting, throwing up their hands or doing all three.

It was chaos.

I stood by one wall and watched it, my insides churning. I had come from a department so civilised that my manager had turned against me because I'd rolled my eyes during a pre-shift meeting. Now I was in a room where everyone seemed to swearing and shouting at the managers, and they didn't seem to be taking any notice. It was more like a teacher and her pre-schoolers than a hotel's housekeeping staff and its management.

I couldn't send back food in a restaurant. How was I going to deal with all *this*?

Since I had never worked in hotel housekeeping before – or in any other kind of housekeeping for that matter; I didn't even do it in my own home – my new bosses thought it prudent to put me through Room

Attendant training first.

I was directed to an office in the bowels of the hotel, where one of the managers was trying to hold down the fort. 'Office' might be a strong word, as it was really just a section of the laundry room that had been partitioned off for her. I was left there, alone, for nearly an hour, with only the smell of detergent to keep me company, before someone finally arrived to tell me to come back tomorrow.

The next morning, I waited in the cafeteria with my fellow trainees: young women brought in from other countries by contractors to work as housekeepers, a whole other world I knew nothing about. One of the women had left her children in Brazil to come to the States and was living in a single hotel room with five other women in a similar position to her. The contractor sent a bus to collect them in the morning and a bus to bring them back at home at night, and if there were any problems at work – under-performance, sick days, etc. – they'd be on a plane back home and in debt to the tune of thousands of dollars in visa fees.

Suddenly, walking to work through Downtown Disney and living in Plantation Park didn't look so bad. I felt ashamed of my complaining.

Training started with a series of videos about things like bed-making and chemical safety, and handouts riddled with misspellings. (Coffee, last time I checked, was spelled with two 'f's.) Then it was up into a guest room to learn the ins and outs of bed making.

I soon realised why the beds were so comfortable and it was the same reason they were a complete pain in the ass to make up: excessive bed linen. There was a mattress pad, two plain sheets, a blanket, a decorative sheet with piping, a down-filled comforter, four pillows, and one decorative cushion. They had to go on in a certain way, in an exact order, tucked correctly and left without a wrinkle in sight. Easier said than done.

But I wasn't supposed to be cleaning or bed-making

– I'd be the one checking that someone else had done it right. After my day of RA training, and now dressed in the Inspector's Costume of black pants and brown shirt and with a Nextel radio clipped to my belt – I'd soon be hearing its *beep beep* in my dreams – I showed up for the Inspectors' pre-shift. It was in the Housekeeping Department's conference room and full of dour faces.

The Inspectors didn't seem interested in talking to each other, let alone me, and so I stood off to one side, feeling uncomfortable and grieving for my beloved Front Desk.

I had no idea how much I was about to miss it.

Fourteen
GO FOR LAUNCH

The dream of seeing a Space Shuttle launch from Cape Canaveral had been around since my *Space Camp* days, and was part of the reason I'd come to Florida in the first place.

There was no greater spectacle on earth than seeing a spaceship depart from it and knowing I was going to be living an hour's drive from the launch pads for eighteen whole months, I figured it would be pretty difficult for me *not* to see one.

But twelve months of bad luck later and still no launch, I was beginning to suspect that I'd accidentally stepped on a crack in the pavement that was directly beneath a ladder a black cat had crossed while smashing a mirror to bits. It was the only plausible explanation for how difficult the universe made it for me to tick this dream off my list.

Launch No. 1: STS-115

I managed to miss my first Shuttle launch just four days after landing in Orlando.

When *Atlantis* blasted off from Cape Canaveral on

September 9th, 2006, I had been growing bored in my Walt Disney World hotel room. Before leaving Ireland I'd looked into the possibility of being there for it, but a 'Launch Day Package' including tickets and transportation was far more than I could afford to spend just four days in and for all I knew I could have been due to start Orientation the very same day. So instead I had consoled myself with the fact that ahead of me were eighteen more months of second chances, and had watched the launch on CNN.

But if I'd known that NASA's first ever alleged astronaut felon was onboard, I might have made more of an effort.

After *Columbia* disintegrated during re-entry on February 1st, 2003, the Space Shuttle program ground to a halt while NASA determined the cause of the tragedy – a foam strike seconds after launch – and worked to prevent it ever happening again. For the crew of STS-115, this cautious postponement put them in the record books for having the longest wait of any crew in NASA history – just under four years between selection and flight.

The media speculated that the stress of this delay could have been a contributing factor when on February 5th, 2007, NASA Astronaut and STS-115 crew member Lisa Nowak was arrested in a parking lot at Orlando International Airport and charged with attempted kidnap and murder. Nowak, a married mother of two, had allegedly viewed her intended victim, Air Force Captain Colleen Shipman, as her rival for the affections of another astronaut, STS-116 crew member William Oefelien.

Wanting to confront Shipman about her relationship with Oefelien, Nowak drove non-stop from Houston, Texas to Orlando; a journey of some 960 miles. Although Nowak claimed she had only intended to frighten Shipman, she happened to be travelling with pepper spray, latex gloves, garbage bags and an eight-inch knife, and was wearing a trench coat and a wig at the time. This bizarre love triangle lit the tabloids ablaze with wry reports – the *New York Post*, for example, called the incident 'a space stalk' and Nowak 'a lovelorn NASA moonbat' - while blood rushed to the cheeks of the Astronaut Office. Worse still, there wasn't a single report that didn't mention how Nowak had reportedly worn diapers (similar to the ones worn by Shuttle crews during launch and re-entry) on her crazed drive from Houston to Orlando; an attempt, apparently, to avoid time-wasting bathroom breaks. It didn't take NASA long to release a curt statement announcing that the alleged bunny-boiling space traveller was no longer in their employ.[4]

But back in September 2006, I was a guest of the Tuna and Nowak was presumably still stable. I had watched the last launch on TV in Holland, and, since then, had managed to close the gap between the Cape and me by more than a few thousand miles, but I was stumped by the last sixty.

Eighteen months, I reminded myself. If NASA kept to their launch schedule then I'd have plenty more chances to see it for real.

The following morning I was leafing through my complimentary copy of *USA Today* while I waited for my chocolate-chip Mickey-shaped pancakes when I got a nasty shock.

Underneath a photo of yesterday's blue sky streaked with familiar smoky trails a caption read, *Disney guests pause in Epcot to watch the launch of Space Shuttle* Atlantis *on STS-115.*

---

[4] On November 10th, 2009, Nowak agreed to a plea deal with prosecutors and pleaded guilty to charges of felony burglary of a car and misdemeanor battery. She denies wearing diapers.

I may have been in awe of its beauty but I had underestimated its scale. With nothing but a flat expanse stretching from here all the way to the Cape, and the Shuttle soaring straight up into space, all I would have needed to do to see it yesterday would have been to walk outside and look up.

Launch No. 2: STS-116

The next launch was to be of the Space Shuttle *Discovery* on December 7th.

For me, the month of December was already a lost cause. Although I was keeping a smile tacked to my face at work I was crying into my ugly Wal-Mart sheets every night, and my first ever Christmas away from home was still to come. But someone was going to try and put a little light in my life: one of my managers, Tracy.

Tracy had grown up in Central Florida and told me about how in her childhood she had watched launches streak up through the sky from her backyard with her father. When she heard about my launch dreams she vowed to help me achieve them because as luck, or lack thereof, would have it, I was scheduled to work with Tracy on the night of December 7th.

Come launch day, I was jittery with nerves, convinced I'd get caught with a guest at the last minute, stuck resolving some inane issue about torn bed linen or a missing remote control while *Discovery* lit up the night sky. But I needn't have worried because Tracy, my self-appointed Shuttle Launch Fairy Godmother, took me off the desk at T-Minus 30 minutes.

Bringing up the NASA website in the back office, my stomach dropped at the news that the Cape's weather was in the red. Unless the heavy band of cloud currently settled over the launch pad buzzed off somewhere else, the launch would be a no-go.

I tried to think positive thoughts. After all, with only

a ninety percent chance that the weather would prevent the launch, there was a whole ten percent chance that the launch would go ahead without a hitch; I focused on that. I was desperate for it to happen – in my delicate emotional state, who knows what sort of affect another disappointment would have on me. I might walk out in front of that Disney bus tomorrow, instead on getting on it.

The countdown continued.

At T-Minus 9 minutes, the sequence entered its final built-in hold and Tracy and I took an elevator to the roof, twelve floors up. Our colleague Claire radioed us with updates and less than five minutes before scheduled launch time, she broke the bad news: inclement weather had forced a scrub.

I was crushed but not surprised. Clearly, the universe was hell bent on screwing me out of every opportunity I had for happiness. Seeing a night launch from the roof of the hotel while the Epcot fireworks exploded in the foreground – yep, that would have been pretty darn fantastic. But instead, I was moping back to the desk with a lump in my throat.

Thank you, universe. Thank you SO very much.

A second attempt to launch *Discovery* was scheduled for 8.47pm the following Saturday but with only a twenty percent chance of favourable weather, I was convinced that this attempt would ultimately be scrubbed as well.

In a cruel yet somehow familiar twist of fate, I had the day off work. But Eva was working, and I didn't yet own a car (or in case you've forgotten, know how to drive one), so it made little difference. In case the universe was listening I pretended I couldn't care less, that I wasn't even aware there was a launch. Or even a Shuttle program, for that matter.

NASA who?

But with thirty minutes to go my curiosity got the

better of me and I went online to see what was happening.

All systems go.

I was devastated.

Were I to have gone outside, I might have been able to at least see the Shuttle's fiery path across the sky. But it was already dark and raining, and once I left the apartment, I wouldn't have any way of knowing what was going on out at the Cape. So I watched yet another Shuttle – and one third of a future astronaut love triangle, William Oefelien – head to space on TV.

And that was the final Space Shuttle-shaped novelty straw.

I already had plenty of good reasons to learn how to drive, but now I had a deadline to go with them.

The next launch – *Atlantis* on STS-117 – was slated for March 15th and I vowed I would drive myself there.

Launch No. 3: STS-117

And I would have been able to, had the launch gone ahead.

But – of *course* – while *Atlantis* waited patiently on the pad, a freak hailstorm descended on the Cape and dented the exposed nose of the Shuttle's External Fuel Tank. The mission was delayed indefinitely while the whole shebang - tank, Orbiter and two Solid Rocket Boosters - was hauled back inside the VAB for repairs.

Yes, a hailstorm over Florida in February.

You couldn't make it up.

At least when *Atlantis* finally did launch nearly three months later on June 8th, I stepped a little bit closer to realising my launch dream. As the 250th manned orbital flight soared into the sky, I followed its trail from the roof of the hotel; my Shuttle Launch Fairy Godmother had succeeded on her second try.

Seconds after launch we spotted it on the horizon,

just above the Marriot Hotel on World Centre Drive, and I got to see a Shuttle stride towards space with my own eyes for the very first time.

Of course she *was* sixty miles to the east and climbing, so we couldn't actually see the vehicle itself. What we were looking at was a bright, burning flame atop a thick rope of smoke, about as big as a pencil might look to you if you held it at arm's length, and you had exceptionally long arms.

But the intellectual knowledge of what it was transformed it into an awesome sight, and left me itching to get out to the Cape. I wanted to close in on those remaining sixty miles.

Launch No. 4: STS-118

I considered requesting the day of the next launch – August 8th – off work, but since I'd spent most of July submitting schedule requests, what with John's visit and my birthday trip to D.C., I thought yet another one would be pushing it, and besides, I happened to have the ninth and tenth off already. All I needed was a little technical glitch or wayward thundercloud to delay it by a day and I'd be free to drive out to the Cape and see it.

I probably don't even need to tell you that the whole operation went off without a hitch and *Endeavour* took off without me. Not only did it go on its very first launch attempt, but it wasn't even delayed by *a single second*.

I was beginning to think I should just abandon all hope. The build up to each launch was like being beaten with excitement, stress and disappointment sticks, then being left in a heap on the floor metaphorically bruised and bloodied, without any payoff. I couldn't take it anymore. Instead of fulfilling my dreams, NASA's Shuttle launch schedule was quickly becoming the thing doctors would be interested in hearing about when they diagnosed my future stomach ulcer or cardiac arrhythmia.

But then the universe decided she'd had her fun. All the planets aligned, a launch day went according to plan and as *Discovery* alighted on mission STS-120, I stood on the banks of the Indian River and watched it happen.

Launch No. 5: STS-120

Space Shuttle *Discovery* was slated for launch at 11.38am on October 22nd, 2007, and Andrea and I headed towards the Cape with hopes of seeing it.

Originally we had intended to get up with the dawn and drive out there on launch morning, figuring that if we were on the road by seven we could avoid the fabled traffic jams of The Launch Day Eastward Exodus. But when we shared this plan with our co-workers, they thought we'd been hitting the crazy pills. Kelly advised us to leave no later than six and Mark recalled traffic backed up all the way into Orlando the last time a Shuttle launched.

Neither Andrea nor I were too keen on getting up in the middle of the night, so at the last minute, we decided to drive out there the night before instead, securing what was surely the last remaining hotel room in the whole of Cocoa Beach.

It seemed like a good idea at the time, having arrived, to then head for the dunes with beer and a box of Oreo Caksters and after that, stay up until four in the morning Googling Taylor Kitsch and *Altar Boyz* videos, but when our wake-up call came only three hours later it suddenly didn't seem like all that wise a move.

Outside it was shaping up to be a beautiful day: sunshine, clear skies, no wind. We flicked through the local news channels until we came across live feed of VIP guests arriving at the Cape ahead of the launch countdown. Among them was *Star Wars* creator George Lucas. Apparently somewhere onboard *Discovery*, the light sabre swung around in *Return of the Jedi* was carefully stowed away. To commemorate the thirtieth anniversary of the original trilogy – and to make the heads of *Star Wars* nerds everywhere spin with delight – the prop was going to visit the International Space Station. Also visiting the ISS was NASA Astronaut Dan Tani who, I would later learn, was married to a Corkonian; back home, the newspapers were filled with stories about the launch.

Most importantly, at T-Minus 3 hours and 30 minutes, we were still go for launch.

After the requisite Starbucks stop – conveniently, our hotel had one in its lobby – we drove the short distance from Cocoa Beach to Titusville, the small town that sits directly across the Indian River from Cape Canaveral, with only a vague notion of what we were going to do once we got there.

Miho (i.e. Original Mirage Owner) had told me once about how she'd watched a launch from the McDonalds on US-1, a highway that ran through Titusville. From there she had had an unobstructed view, almost directly opposite the VAB.

Naturally we weren't the only ones with that bright idea. A mile out, cars and trucks ahead of us began pulling off the road and nudging their way into every available space to the east of US-1 and the McDonald's lot was already full.

We were wondering what to do next just as we came upon the riverside parking lot of a restaurant called 'Paul's Smokehouse' where spaces were going for ten bucks a pop. It looked like a pleasant place to wait out the morning and it was probably as good or better than anything else we were likely to find further down, so we handed over ten dollars and took up a spot.

By T-Minus 2 hours 30 minutes, we had secured a prime viewing position at the water's edge. It was a little bit closer to a couple of fire ant hills than I liked but it was going to be a great place to watch the launch, if it went ahead.

I asked the universe to please, *please* let me see it happen.

Then all there was to do was sit and wait.

At T-Minus 2 hours, we take a stroll back up the street to McDonalds to get some greasy plastic for breakfast. A couple of kindly senior citizens astute enough to have brought deck-chairs agree to watch our spot for us while we're gone.

T-Minus 1 hour 40 minutes. Andrea and I exchange looks that go some way to convey how much we want to throttle the two little blonde girls to the left of us. They are unrelenting in their test of their grandmother's patience, asking an endless barrage of stupid questions in whiney voices. 'What's *taking* so long? Why are we *waiting*? What's wrong with your *face*?'

T-Minus 1 hour 15 minutes. I remember that somewhere in my car is a newspaper so now at least one of us has some reading material with which to pass the time. Hungry creepy-crawlies are making their way into our McDonald's leftovers.

T-Minus 1 hour. We stifle laughter as one of the aforementioned senior citizens warns her one hundredth idiot about the fire ants. Every few minutes someone goes to sit on the patch of empty grass between us and these ladies, thinking they are the first ones to notice this vacant viewing spot.

T-Minus 45 minutes. 'Be careful – that's an ant hill.'

T-Minus 39 minutes. 'Take care there, there's an ant hill.'

T-Minus 32 minutes. 'GET OFF THAT DAMN ANT HILL!'

T-Minus 30 minutes. A couple of hundred people are now gathered in the parking lot of Paul's Smokehouse. (At $10 a car, Paul must be *raking* it in.) A text message arrives from my mum – she's out shopping, nowhere

194

near a TV or radio and therefore really of no use to us at this important juncture. If I'd been thinking clearly I could have had her installed in front of Sky News, sending me text message updates at regular intervals.

T-Minus 25 minutes. Some guy has a radio. He stands in the middle of the crowd holding it aloft so everyone can hear NASA's tinny chatter from across the river. After a few minutes you can totally tell his arm is killing him, but he can't put it down now. I notice my shoulders are hot to the touch and turning a shade of Lobster Fusion 104. Anyone got some sunscreen?

T-Minus 15 minutes. One small, solitary cloud appears out of nowhere and settles itself directly above where I think the Shuttle is. I overhear someone saying there is a concern about ice on the launch pad, even though this is Central Florida in October and the temperature's about eighty degrees.

T-Minus 12 minutes. I fetch my NASA baseball cap from the car and prepare to be disappointed. My stomach commences its Olympic tumbling routine.

T-Minus 10 minutes. My palms start to sweat. I wait for someone, somewhere, to tell me the launch has been scrubbed. Is it really possible that this will actually go ahead, that in a few short moments, a lifelong dream of mine will be realised? I can't help but doubt it.

Besides the annoying children and the odd NASA voice from the radio, it's all quiet here at the water's edge. A few years previously I had seen the Knicks play at Madison Square Garden and for the whole of the first quarter, I had had the strange feeling that something was very wrong. It was only afterwards I realised what it was: having never before seen a game that wasn't on TV, I was missing the running commentary. It was the same here on the banks of the Indian River. No doubt the launch complex, across from us on the horizon, was a hive of activity. I just hoped that none of it was going to result in the postponement of this launch.

A woman who'd been sitting next to Andrea asked

her if it was okay to take our photo as we watched the launch. Andrea was wearing sunglasses and the woman explained she'd always wanted to get a photo of a launch reflected in a spectator's shades. We hurriedly nodded our agreement and turned back to the countdown.

At T-Minus 3 minutes, I start to lose it. I suddenly realised that I hadn't just been sunbathing all morning, but awaiting a Space Shuttle launch. I'd been thinking *at least last night was fun* and thereby consoling myself that it hadn't been a complete waste of a trip. The two-minute point passed and then unbelievably, the one-minute mark. I looked to Andrea. I looked to the guy with the radio. I looked to my phone. I looked to anyone for news that this countdown had come grinding to a sudden halt.

T-Minus 30 seconds came and went. The clock kept ticking.

I began to panic. I wanted them all to stop, to wait a minute while I savoured this, to just *slow down a second* so I could take it in.

But it didn't stop. It carried on.

I'd been expecting another disappointment; I hadn't prepared for a success.

And so now, I was going to hyperventilate.

I closed my eyes.

When someone began counting down in seconds, I opened them again.

Ten, nine, eight...the crowd at Paul's Smokehouse were on their feet...*seven, six*...a few voices joined in, amplifying it... *five, four*...a lump in my throat...*three*...here come the waterworks...*two*...

Was I really going to see this?

One.

There was a beat.

Then someone shouted, 'There it is!'

Across the river from us, a flame the size of a building was burning bright. Alongside it on the flat horizon, huge billows of smoke sprang out on either side and started to swell.

Discovery was go for launch.

The fire began to rise.

Within seconds it was higher than the roof of the VAB and climbing. After disappearing into a patch of cloud, it emerged on the other side and proceeded to burn a hazy arc, up and away from us as the earth turned, white smoke on a blue sky.

The crowd cheered and applauded, encouraging the ship and its astronaut crew to '*Go, go, go!*' It seemed so impossible. It was frightening. Could this thing really burn its way up into space? We tried to help it along. We willed it towards the stars with our hearts.

A loud rumble came thundering across the Indian River, passed through our chests and then faded away behind us: the launch soundtrack on delay.

My phone beeped with a text message from my mother who had evidently heard the good news: 'LIFT OFF!' Either she was as excited about it as I was or she didn't know how to switch to lower case.

It takes eight minutes for a Space Shuttle to carry its crew into space and for a lot of that time it's visible in some form from the ground. No one moved until the Shuttle became a tiny white dot and then faded completely from sight.

The Space Shuttle was in space.

Sunlight shone on the bright white tendril of smoke left behind in the sky, a reminder that we hadn't merely dreamed the entire thing. It had really happened. We had just seen a spaceship depart from the earth.

And somewhere inside the Orbiter, just above the blaze, seven people – and one light sabre – were going up there with it.

When I came back down to earth myself, I realised I'd been crying the entire time, and not just delicate, single-tear-escapes-down-cheek crying, but great blubbering sobs of irrepressible emotion. I was officially a mess.

Andrea thought my overreaction was hilarious but even she had to admit it had been a hugely moving experience. It was just worse for me due to the whole Shuttle launch dream business and the fact that I cried at the drop of a hat. (I didn't just cry at *Oprah*, I cried at the sixty second promo for *Oprah*.) The dreams of thousands of people had carried that Shuttle into space and, by being here, I had seen one of my own dreams realised as well.

When *Discovery* had disappeared, the woman who'd wanted to take our photo introduced herself as the editor of a local Brevard County newspaper. *Now* we were paying attention. She wrote down our names and where we hailed from, whilst I hoped against hope that nowhere on her memory card was a photo of an overly-emotional sunburned Irish girl with no make-up, three hours' sleep, and all her hair tucked up under a NASA baseball cap.

I rang my Mum to relay the details and started crying all over again, which wasn't a good thing because by then I was at the wheel of the Mirage and on the way home. Mark called from his shift at the desk to say he'd heard it had launched and congratulated me on finally getting to see it. Only then did it begin to sink in.

I've seen a Shuttle launch!

On the way back to Orlando, we rolled down the windows and turned up the radio. Life was good. Yet another dream had been crossed off the list; I needed to get some new ones. Poor Andrea had to be in work by three but as I had the day off, I was free to go home and get back into bed.

However, I was way too jacked up on adrenaline to close my eyes for any length of time. Instead, I replayed my launch video.

A few times.

Okay; over and over for the rest of the day. Happy now?

Two weeks later, I drove back out to Titusville to pick up a copy of the illustrious *North Brevard Beacon*, the editor of which we'd met at the launch.

When I finally located a few copies in a deserted mall not far from Paul's Smokehouse, I laughed out loud.

On the front page and under the heading 'Enlightened Discovery' (clever!), a NASA-capped crying Irish girl held a hand to her heart, face lifted towards the same unseen sight as everyone else around her.

The caption read, '*Standing on the banks of the Indian River near Paul's Smokehouse, Catherine Ryan Howard from Cork, Ireland, is overcome with emotion as she watches Space Shuttle* Discovery *STS-120 lifting into orbit on 22nd October. She said her first launch was the most amazing thing she had ever seen.*'

Fifteen
IN GOD WE TRUST

One day, when I was twelve years old, I stopped believing in God.

I remember the exact moment it happened. Mrs Moran's Sixth Class was preparing for Confirmation and I was sitting in the middle of the room a row away from the teacher, dressed in an itchy green uniform and with my religion textbook open on my desk. As part of our Confirmation preparation, we had to learn a series of questions and answers about the Bible off by heart so that, in a few weeks time, the parish priest could visit us in class and quiz each of us individually. Word on the playground was that if you didn't get your answer right, you wouldn't be allowed make your Confirmation any time this side of Judgment Day.

Today's question was about creation, specifically God's seven-day DIY plan for the world and everything in it. But I was a tad confused, because nowhere in the Book of Genesis was there any mention of dinosaurs.

According to the Bible, in the beginning there was nothing at all, apart from God of course, who had always been and always would be; but he must have been bored off his head because there was no existence. Like, at all. So then God – due to the boredom, I'd say – created the world and everything in it. If you followed the story from the Garden of Eden you would eventually find yourself within reach of historical record, ignoring a few, ahem, gaps.

So where had all the dinosaurs gone?

Back then all I knew about evolution was that it provided a scientific explanation of our origins whose evidence we could actually see and that it had something to do with monkeys. As for my dino data, *Jurassic Park* had come out two summers before. I'd even seen dinosaur fossils with my very own eyes.

But now here was Mrs Moran, who I trusted implicitly, telling me that creation was true, when surely she must also know about dinosaurs and evolution and stuff. (She had to; teachers knew *everything*). I couldn't master the black belt in Doublethink that would have been required to hold both contradictory ideas in my mind at once and believe both to be true, so I made a face.

Right at that moment, Mrs Moran looked directly at me, bore her eyes deep down into my soul – whose existence was now called into question – and said, 'Of course, we know now that it wasn't *literally* seven days. Each day represents hundreds of thousands of years.'

We know now. An innocent phrase that probably flew past my Catholicised classmates without encountering any air resistance, but those three words punched me in my gut with such a force that here I am, recalling them for you fifteen years later. (And also, hundreds of thousands of years? Just how slow *was* this God guy?) Here was the Church with their beloved tale of creation on one hand, and here were hundreds of thousands of dinosaur bones on the other. Faced with hard evidence that Mr Genesis had had a bit of an over-active imagination, they changed their tune and tried to fit the two narratives together even though it was like trying to fit a square peg into a heptagonal hole that's half a foot smaller than the peg in diameter.

To a child, each day of God's Busiest Week actually representing aeons of evolutionary history wasn't all that much of a mind-meld – I'd buy it, for now. But it was all just sounding a little bit too convenient for my liking. Who was to say that if something else showed up tomorrow – an advanced alien race coming to see how their experiment was doing, for instance (I was in my ufology phase at the time) – the Pope wouldn't just shrug, hold up his hands and say, 'Sorry, guys. My bad.'

Up until that point – all of twelve years – I'd been a good little Catholic girl, apart from all the lying. I didn't even know there was such a thing as an Atheist - I didn't know people had the option. Both sides of my family were religious and so off the lot of us went every Sunday morning to Mass. There was a crucifix above my parents' bed, a Holy Water font inside our front door and a letter holder with a hologram of The Last Supper on it, that's still downstairs in the kitchen as I sit here and type these words.

But it wasn't like all my friends and their families weren't in the same ark. It was just the way it was and that was that. It would have never even occurred to me to question it.

That is, if it hadn't been for the *Collins Illustrated Children's Bible* my mother bought me.

It was a thick hardback with a richly illustrated text that had been sanitised enough for kids to read while still retaining all the good stuff like the almighty wrath of God, His endless demands for human sacrifices and all the best plagues and punishments. There exists (like science exists, not Bible exists) a photo of me reading this Bible while on holidays in Benodet, France.

Look at our little pious princess, my parents must have thought to themselves, while I wondered just where Cain's wife had come from.

(I'm *still* wondering that. Anyone know?)

Of course at the time – I was about seven or eight then – these little...discrepancies, shall we say, didn't really bother Child Me. I went to Mass every Sunday and six days a week during Lent, and I dutifully said my prayers every night for fear I wouldn't wake up again if I didn't. After my grandfather died when I was eleven, I happily chatted away to him at night in the dark for several weeks, asking him to keep everyone safe and apologising for any bad-word-saying or little-white-lie telling he may have been witness to earlier.

If I did have any questions or confusions about God or the Bible, there wasn't really anyone I could ask. My father flat-out refused to entertain any questioning of religion whatsoever ('Don't be talking rubbish!' was his refrain of choice whenever I brought up things like why, for example, it was now suddenly okay to go to Mass on Saturday night) and my mother's response was to roll her eyes and say I thought too much about these things while simultaneously pushing me outside to play.

When dictionaries were added to our book list for school, I discovered a word that might describe me. After the initial novelty of looking up swear words wore off, I looked up the term 'agnostic'; I'd heard it used on TV – oh, the root of all evil! – to describe someone who wasn't religious. I thought it kind of sounded like me, a person who wasn't too sure either way. But eleven-year-old girls don't tend to announce at the dinner table (or eating off their lap in front of the TV, in my case) that they're agnostic, so I just kept quiet and said my prayers instead.

After all, this could be a test.

But a year later, the dinosaurs were a deal breaker. I went ahead and made my Confirmation in March 1995, even though I seriously considered putting my hand up and saying, 'Ah, *actually*...' It bothered me; the whole point of Confirmation was to confirm your faith in God for the first time since you were – according to the Church - old enough to understand what it was you were doing- but I was old enough, ironically, to be starting to think that the whole thing was about as believable as Michael Jackson saying he'd never had plastic surgery.

By the time I began secondary school at the end of that summer, I was officially an atheist. Well, you know what I mean – it wasn't like there was a place I had to go register or anything. I didn't believe in God – I couldn't. Today I still don't, and I know I never will.

So what was I doing buying a ticket to The Holy Land Experience, Orlando's – and possibly the world's – only religious theme park, where Jesus himself was the star of the 3 o'clock parade?

As I walked past a security guard dressed as a centurion and into what the guide called the 'Jerusalem Street Market', having shelled out thirty dollars for an admission ticket, I began to ask myself the very same thing.

Before I moved to the United States, I considered myself to be a quiet but dedicated atheist.

Other than my immediate family, I never announced to anyone that I didn't believe in God unless I was asked directly. Many of my extended family only found out about my atheism a couple of minutes ago; and a few of them – and one Ms Desmond - will be particularly surprised to learn that by the time I travelled to the shrine of Lourdes in France to be a helper of the sick, I'd already been a fully-fledged Non-Believer for more than three years.

But now that being a militant atheist has become popular of late, we and other freethinkers like us are under attack stateside by a moral majority gone mad.

You may not associate Florida with the rednecks and Bible thumpers of the Deep South, but Florida is more southern than any of them. You don't have to drive too far outside Orlando's city limits before you encounter billboards insisting that abortion is murder and damning all homosexuals to hell.

For weeks, the headline on the local news had centred around a new fight to keep evolution out of schools. After a prolonged and heated debate, it had been agreed that evolution could be taught alongside creationism, but only if it was called 'the scientific theory of evolution' when presented to the children. What *wouldn't* be explained to the children, however, is that in science, the word 'theory' doesn't mean a speculative idea but an explanation that has been built on quantifiable evidence and exhaustively subjected to scrutiny, challenge and test.

It is quite unlike, for example, the religious 'theory' that the flood which had Noah running off to Home Depot for wood and nails was also responsible for laying down that troublesome fossil record – in this case, 'theory' seems to mean 'desperate but amusing cover story to dispel the notion that Mr T-Rex isn't in the Bible only because the fantasists who wrote it had no possible way of knowing that he had ever walked the earth'.

In the run up to my first stateside Christmas, all that self-proclaimed 'traditionalist' Bill O'Reilly and his Fox News friends were banging on about was the so-called 'War on Christmas'. Non-Christians had banded together to launch a full-scale attack on Christmas trees, fairy lights and sales clerks saying 'Merry Christmas' when they handed you your change. This got the Christian Right's matronly underwear in a twist because, damn it, they didn't want to be told to have a 'Happy Holidays'. They figured that despite having a Constitution which guarantees religious freedom for all religious denominations and not just for Christians, when it came to Christmas everyone else could put up or shut up. They weren't prepared to make any concessions, even during the season of good will towards men.

Ironic really, since even the Church knows that 25th December isn't JC's birthday and that the date originated from the Pagan period of worship that followed the Winter Solstice.

And what about the rights of the American citizens who don't believe in God but have to see the words 'In

God We Trust' on the back of every dollar bill? Will the Christian Right rise up to fight that battle for religious freedom?

When I heard that Kirk Cameron, Eighties TV star and former teen heartthrob, was a presenter on one of the Christian channels, I had to take a look and boy, was I sorry I did.

According to my cable guide, the show was a televangical version of *60 Minutes*. It opened with Cameron, looking as cute as he had done back when I'd been glued to his sitcom, *Growing Pains*, walking slowly down some steps with a clipboard and telling the following story:

Somewhere in the States there was a firehouse, and this firehouse had a fireman. In an attempt to impress the fire chief and the rest of his brigade, this fireman purchased a state of the art sound system for one of the fire trucks. He was fiddling with it in the truck's cab when a call came in of a serious fire, and he continued to fiddle with it for several minutes while somewhere a person burned to death waiting for him.

Cameron went on about how the fireman had been charged with negligence or something, and of course had been fired from his job as a fireman. Then he looked straight into the camera and said that if you don't constantly try to spread your faith by converting everyone around you, then you are just like that fireman, sitting in the truck doing nothing while someone burns to death.

This, ladies and gentlemen, was religion in America.

So when I saw a sign for The Holy Land Experience, owned by the Christian Trinity Broadcasting Network (TBN), I just had to stop by for a visit. I wanted to know what a religious theme park looked like. How could you make the Bible, with all its fire and brimstone and judgment, fun enough to be worth paying thirty dollars to experience? What kind of people, besides undercover atheists like me, went there on vacation?

And perhaps most importantly of all, what kind of things, other than Bibles, did they sell in the gift shop?

The Holy Land Experience is just off I-4, directly opposite the Mall at Millennia. Andrea often joked about the signage that pointed towards the mall in one direction and to The Holy Land Experience in the other, when, really, religious-like rapture could be had at both.

As I looked for a spot in the parking lot, I realised I was nervous. Would they be able to tell that I was only here to determine how crazy they were on a scale of one to ten? Would my skin start to singe as soon as I walked through the gates? Would they try to convert me? The website warned that The Holy Land strived to promote a family friendly environment (that was fine – the very same line was on Magic Kingdom maps) that glorified God (uh-oh). It also said that for safety reasons, only Holy Land Experience employees could dress in costume. Well gosh darn it, I'd have to leave my Mary Magdalene outfit at home.

I bought my admission ticket from a man dressed in decidedly Biblical-looking robes. Next to him, a sign advertised The Holy Land's version of an annual pass, the Jerusalem Gold Annual Membership.

'That ticket is good for another seven days,' he told me. 'Enjoy your visit. Be blessed.'

I thanked him and faked a smile. The entrance was like something from a Medieval Times restaurant, but I think it was supposed to be reminiscent of Jerusalem. Ah, yes – my Discovery Guide (read: park map) said it was modelled after the Damascus and Jaffa Gates. How wonderful. The ticket-taker was a skirt-wearing centurion who was chatting happily with a girl dressed in a long robe and wearing a headdress, even though it was at least seventy-five degrees in the shade.

'Be blessed,' they told me in unison. Evidently 'be blessed' was the same as the 'Have a Magical Day' I was obligated to say back in Walt Disney World. I had just found a job worse than being an It's A Small World operator.

Just beyond the gates was a small market with a couple of colourful stalls and some more robed girls. A few visitors were resting on benches, drinking coffee. That seemed like a pretty good place to start - I was going to need a good shot of caffeine to get through this, if not something stronger.

I followed the smell into the Sycamore Tree Coffee Shop and got myself the biggest latte they'd let me have. The guy ahead of me in the queue was kind of cute, but before that thought could go any further, I remembered where I was. Unless he was also an Undercover Atheist, I didn't think it would work out somehow.

As I looked for the sugar, I spotted a couple of shelves towards the back of the café that were stocked with Bible Bread. What the hell was Bible Bread? It looked like thick Melba toast, and was apparently imported from Israel. Next to the bread were small tins of Scripture Mints - just plain mints, but under the lid of each tin was a piece of scripture. Perfect for that bad breath/crisis of faith situation.

It was another beautiful Florida day, so I took my coffee and my growing horror into the KidVenture plaza, a playground built around the story of Noah's Ark and including a rather threatening-looking plastic wave. I sat there for a while and watched other visitors walk through, keeping my eyes peeled for a cross-shaped handbag or a bracelet engraved with 'WWJD?', but they all seemed pretty normal to me. Outwardly, at least.

I passed by something called The Wilderness Tabernacle ('Behold the High Priest as he takes you on a journey through Israel's ancient priesthood, culminating with the glory of God revealed above the Ark of the Covenant') and a replica of the caves where the Dead Sea Scrolls were discovered.

I mean, really - replica *caves*? It was like something

out of an episode of *Father Ted*.

I was thinking about how The Holy Land Experience badly needed to get some Disney Imagineers and fast, when I almost tripped over the Ten Commandments. They were reproduced on two stone tablets that looked unfortunately like cartoon headstones. I had been wondering how far I'd get before running into those.

Signs directed me to a theatre presentation called 'The Seed of Promise', showing every thirty minutes in the Theatre of Life. This 'inspiring film' had something to do with a cute lamb and the Big Man's action plan for saving all our sorry souls. Parental guidance was advised due to the 'realism' of some scenes. Of course, the Bible was the perfect bedtime story, what with its depths of fiery hell, murder by brick and unbaptised babies in limbo.

I decided I was already sufficiently inspired and moved on.

Next up was the impressive Temple Plaza, a huge white and gold temple/theatre, six storeys high and visible from I-4. In the glare of the mid-afternoon sun, the white marble was practically blinding. The guide claimed that the temple was 'the centre of Jerusalem's religious life' and that they now used this replica of it to stage musicals. On the temple steps/stage, more robed figures looked to be setting up for a show, but not even for the sake of my investigative report could I stomach that, so I high-tailed it out of there instead.

There was one thing I actually *did* want to see: the world's largest indoor model of Jerusalem in A.D. 66, but unfortunately presentations had ended for the day. All I could do was look at a picture of it on the sign outside, and wonder how many other indoor models of Jerusalem in A.D. 66 it had had to compete with for that title.

A large lake takes up a good portion of the grounds and now I took a seat at its edge to make some notes and sip some water. The guidebook *had* warned that a visit to The Holy Land Experience could leave visitors 'parched.'

At least the park had a nice atmosphere - its visitors were quiet and respectful, the way I would be in a library. There weren't even any kids running about. I was starting to think this was at least a nice place to stroll around for a couple of hours until I looked across the lake and saw that the bushes had been cut into letters and read 'He Is Risen'.

I was risen too, right out of my seat.

Moving on.

The jewel in the park's Christ-loving crown is the multi-million dollar 'Scriptorium', an extensive exhibit or 'Centre for Biblical Antiquities' that explains how we got the Bible and takes nearly an hour to fully tour. I genuinely wanted to know where the Bible came from, so off I went.

Not unlike Stitch's Great Escape at Magic Kingdom, the Scriptorium doesn't let you leave until the show is over. A guide gives you a five-minute overview before you are left inside (after a 'Be Blessed', of course) with an elderly couple, two teenage boys and your own regret.

Touring the Scriptorium is an automated affair, and it's actually quite well orchestrated. As you move from room to room, an audio track explains what you're looking at, and lighting changes highlight the item the disembodied voice of the narrator is currently talking about. When the lights dim in the current room and illuminate in the next one, you know it's time to move on.

But that's all the praise I'm willing to give it. The guide promised the Scriptorium contained 'authentic, and ancient artifacts' – and that horribly incorrect use of a comma was all theirs - but all I could see were some old Bibles and a printing press. Yes, they did explain how the Bible had spread through society to become today's ultimate bestseller, but they didn't seem concerned with where it had come from in the first place. I had wanted to see God's first draft, double spaced and corrected with red biro. It was like a history of Irish dancing that began with Michael Flatley.

I was also getting sick of the phrase 'independently confirmed'. Everywhere I turned in The Holy Land Experience, things were being independently confirmed – a historical Jesus, his miraculous and impossible resurrection, and ultimately, the existence of God himself. It was a veritable spree of independent confirmations, but no information was forthcoming about exactly who was doing the confirming, or how. But I guess there was no need, this being the quintessential act of preaching to the choir.

I was initially confused by the final room on the Scriptorium tour, because it was just a living room. I thought for a second that we had accidentally wandered into a staff area or someone's home, but then the narration began, and I got it; the living room had a television, a computer, a stereo system and some video games, and was supposed to show that the modern world is nothing but one big distraction from God.

It was nice to feel the sun on my face again after an hour of being bashed with a Bible. I walked past the Oasis Palms Café - I didn't know there had been hot dogs in biblical times - to get to what was perhaps the most disturbing feature of the park: a full-scale replica of Calvary's Garden Tomb, complete with rolled back tombstone and three wooden crosses on the hill above it. The park map invited me to 'spend time reflecting, praying and enjoying [the] live presentations'. This must have been the site of the park's infamous mid-afternoon performance of The Passion of the Christ: The Child-Friendly Theme Park Edition, although it seemed that all religious reenactments were finished for the day. I would just have to make do with being completely freaked out instead.

No theme park or attraction visit is complete without a look around the gift shop, so I stopped at The Old Scroll Shop to see what was on offer. Inside, I found lots of wood. There were wood-covered Bibles, wooden crosses, wooden ashtrays, wooden pieces of wood - all claiming to have been made in Israel. There were souvenir Holy Land Experience T-shirts and mugs, the New Testament on CD, erasers in the shape of Bibles, and rulers reminding everyone that 'God Wrote a Book.' At least half the store was filled with tie-in merchandise from *The Chronicles of Narnia*, a story I had loved as a child but which was now evidently ruined for me forever. I almost laughed out loud at the tambourines in the shape of the Star of David, and realised that the time had come to leave.

'Thanks for coming,' the Centurion said as I left. 'Be blessed.'

When people of faith discover that you're an atheist, they inevitably adopt a tone of two parts incredulity and three parts condescension and demand that you explain, as a supposed spokesperson for All of Science, what they consider to be the great mysteries of the universe.

'So where do you think we came from, then?'

'What about all the miracles?'

'What about people who've died and seen a bright white tunnel with their loved ones at the end of it?'

'How do you know what's right and what's wrong?'

'If there is no God, then what's it all for?'

I can't really answer these questions, although I'll try: See The Big Bang, primordial soup and evolution for question one; I'll start taking miracles seriously when someone miraculously regenerates an amputated limb; no one who has actually died for real, i.e. died and stayed that way, has been able to tell us about bright lights, tunnels, etc. and these images could well be the hallucinations or symptoms of a dying brain; are you saying that the only reason you don't rape or murder is because you fear the judgment of God if he caught you doing it?; it's for *life*, to see the world and everything in it, to be lucky enough to be here feeling the full spectrum of the human experience - love, joy, friendship - for as long as it lasts. More to the point, I don't *need* to answer them, because I don't believe in anything. I'm not the one carrying the burden of proof.

If I came to you and said that last night three little green men flew in through my bedroom window, abducted me and took me aboard their alien mothership for an unpleasant medical exam and you said it was a dream I had, on whom would be the onus to prove they were telling the truth?

Just because many people believe a particular thing and it has been believed for a long, long time, doesn't make it fact. There was a time when everyone on earth, including its greatest minds, believed it was flat.

Moreover, I don't *want* to talk about it. Asking me to talk about religion is like asking me to talk about my career in the army – neither of them exist in my life, so why even ask?

The only other thing I will say about this atheist business is that the contempt, hatred and scorn directed towards us scares and upsets me. Professor Richard Dawkins, author of *The God Delusion*, regularly gets death threats – which doesn't seem very Christian to me – and there's many a 'F*%k Atheists' group on Facebook and in real life.

But why?

People of faith seem to think that atheists can't be anything other than blasphemous sinners who habitually lie, swear, cheat, steal, drink, take drugs, have sex before marriage, work on Sundays and kill people. But we're not evil. We're as good if not better than our religious equivalents.

I know that I, for one, am just *lovely*.

Sixteen
FAREWELL

My last three months in Orlando passed by in a blur.

I think the fact that I spent them working in Housekeeping may have had something to do with it – it made me wish my remaining Florida days away.

Being an inherently lazy, messy person, the position of Housekeeping Inspector was a bad fit from the start. Factor in eight-hour stretches of non-stop running, Room Attendants who hated me with a vengeance (and with whom I had not one language in common) and the relentless beeping of Nextel radios, and I had myself a job I couldn't do very well and hated intensely.

Despite my teenage fantasies of Ebola hunting in equatorial Africa, I had grown up to be a desk person, thanks in no small part to my love of stationery, spreadsheets and sitting. Also, at a desk, you could drink a lot more coffee.

What I really didn't like was inspecting the underside of toilet bowls while on my hands and knees, emptying trash cans filled with putrefying dirty diapers and having no choice but to put up with verbal abuse from my male subordinates because it wasn't their fault that in their culture, women weren't respected.

The only things that got me through each day were

the coffees I drank almost on the hour, every hour, and the club sandwich at Quizno's I knew I was going to buy myself on the way home. Plus, the job *was* good exercise.

One morning I was called to a room where I deduced that the previous night, a guest had been lying in one of the beds when they felt the need to lift their head and projectile vomit right across the room. By the time I got there, it had dried on the floor, all over the other bed and was coating the night stand.

This was what the Mouse called 'a protein spill', and since only inspectors had access to the equipment needed to handle such things, the mess was mine to clean up.

At some point in the operation, I happened to look up and see myself in the mirror above the armoire, wearing a mask and latex gloves, stuffing a sheet heavy with a stranger's regurgitated dinner into a biohazard bag, all the while being careful to breathe through my mouth and earning ten dollars an hour for the privilege.

Is this what I'd come to Florida for?

I often thought back to that night in Holland almost two years before when Kelly offered me the job over the phone. I had been so excited I could barely breathe. When I called my family back home in Ireland just minutes after I got the news, I struggled to get out the words and gulp down air at the same time. I thought my life was about to change; nothing would be the same after this. Back then, 'February 2008' was so far in the future it sounded foreign on the tongue. Now it was only a few weeks away and getting closer by the day.

I couldn't decide if I was happy to be leaving or happy to be going home, so I took going home out of the equation.

When Sheelagh (the Best Friend, if you've forgotten) told me she was going backpacking in Central America, I invited myself along. We planned for her to come here first for a week and then we'd fly to Guatemala City to begin our nine-week adventure. Neither of us had ever been backpacking before and so, gripped with excitement, we started working out our itinerary in emails filled with smiley faces and superfluous exclamation marks.

Whilst my Disney experience hurtled towards its end, I distracted myself with thoughts of Guatemalan volcanoes, malaria pills, and the Lonely Planet's *Central America on a Shoestring*.

So now I was just happy to be leaving.

The same Claire who had told me about Jellyrolls had also warned me against leaving everything until the last minute. 'You think you've got loads of time left,' she had said, 'but it's over before you know it.' With this in mind I threw myself into a hectic schedule of activities in the hope that I could cross most if not all of the items off my To Do Before I Leave Florida list before I did.

We celebrated Andrea's birthday with at day at Epcot, using its Food and Wine Festival as an excuse to drink our way around the world (check!), while Andrea's birthday badge earned her a free cookie and upwards of thirty birthday greetings throughout the day (Cast Members always respond to a birthday badge with a 'Happy Birthday!'). Halloween weekend found me in her hometown of Lakeland for the first time (check!), pretty much appropriately attired for a showing of *The Rocky Horror Picture Show* (check!). I toured the brand new Ikea on Conroy Road (check!) and saw the Apollo documentary *In the Shadow of the Moon* (check!) at the Enzian Theatre in Maitland. We used our hospitality passes to check out Westside's Disney Quest arcade (check! And don't bother!) as well as the nightclubs of Pleasure Island (check!). When Christmas came around again, I went to my second Mickey's Very Merry Christmas Party (check!) and saw the Osborne Family Lights at Disney-MGM Studios, where on the same night I finally caught a performance of their closing show, Fantasmic (check and check!).

Meanwhile I slogged through my days in the Housekeeping Department, although working there did have one major benefit befitting of my imminent departure. Although it usually left me too tired to muster the energy required to leave my apartment, working a day shift did help me see a lot more of my friends. We formed a lunchtime gang: my Scandal Sisters from Front Desk, Will, Mark and Charles, and Ray, a fellow former Front Desker who had also just become an inspector, making me feel less alone in the department. Often our little chinwag was the highlight of my day.

Well, that and all the free coffee.

To be fair, Housekeeping did have its attractions. Having realised that I was not just visiting the department but there to stay – at least for a few months, anyway – the other inspectors had started to talk to me, and within a few weeks I was as close to being one of them as I was going to get. We felt like a team, more so than I'd ever experienced back at Front Desk. There was camaraderie here; it was like every day we fought a common enemy – 1,509 dirty rooms – and the only way to win was to fight it together. Inspectors frequently stayed late to help out other inspectors and even as you went up the ranks, there was far less of an 'us versus them' attitude than there seemed to be elsewhere in the hotel. Everybody just rolled up their sleeves and got on with it, no matter what their title - even the Director of Housekeeping herself got down on her knees to clean toilet bowls. I may have been utterly spent at the end of every day, but I also felt like I'd actually accomplished something – I'd got my floor clean.

On my last day as a Housekeeping Inspector – my last day working at the hotel – the entire team was called to the conference room for a mysterious meeting. No gathering of the inspectors was complete without an earful about something or other, so this news wasn't exactly welcomed as it beeped its way out of our Nextels. But once we were all sat down, the managers brought out a cake whose sugar content could induce diabetic shock and presented me with a good-bye gift: a travel mug with a bleary-eyed Minnie Mouse on it, holding a cup of coffee under a caption that read, 'Mornings ain't pretty'.

Clearly my monumental caffeine consumption hadn't gone unnoticed.

As everyone wished me luck with my travels and beyond, I was as surprised as anyone that despite my months of complaining, moaning and criticising, I was a little bit sad to be leaving Housekeeping behind me.

A *very* little bit.

Sheelagh arrived in Orlando on February 21st.

Picking her up at the airport, the first thing I did was make her promise she wouldn't make fun of my pseudo-American accent. I didn't sound like I was from Ireland anymore, but I didn't sound like I was from Orlando either. I'd somehow managed to develop a mid-Atlantic accent all of my own. My excuse was that I'd an exceptionally good ear, and I was sticking with it.

Although I was ecstatic to show my best friend Orlando and all of my life there, the week was tinged with sadness. It was my last week of living in Florida, the end of my eighteen-month Disney World experience. I had thought I was ready to leave Orlando, but now I wasn't so sure.

I loved the sunshine, the beach, the malls, the people. I loved that I lived so close to Disney World and only an hour away from Kennedy Space Centre. I loved that I could pop into Celebration for breakfast. I loved that behind my apartment was a crystal blue swimming pool alongside which I could spend any morning, and I loved that Orlando had a Starbucks on every corner.

Or in every strip mall.

I loved that I had been able to have all sorts of adventures. I'd had Sunday brunch in Georgetown and seen a Shuttle launch into space. In my last few weeks,

I'd also seen the Christmas tree outside Rockefeller Centre in New York City, been to Mardi Gras in New Orleans, and even attended a screening of John Cusack's new movie *Grace is Gone* at Downtown Disney, with John Cusack himself in attendance. I loved having a car and I loved driving it past fireworks on the way home from work. I loved that every time my friends and I went inside a Disney park, we had no reason to believe it would be for the last time.

But equally, I sometimes feared that I was living in a kind of suspended animation. Disney World and Orlando tended to be a magnet for people who never wanted to grow up, a kind of Neverland for college grads who sought no more substance in life than a nice car and a good time on Saturday night. I thought I needed more than that. Even if I had been legally able to stay in Orlando, what would I have done? Stayed at my job at the hotel, driving in and out each day, breaking up the monotony with beach parties, trips to the mall and days at the parks? Would that life keep me happy?

Orlando had been nice while it lasted, but there was no long-term future for me here. The place didn't seem to offer a future for anyone; it was merely a playground we all stopped at to have some fun on our way to somewhere else.

But then as my last week drew to a close I began to panic, thinking that I was searching for things that weren't even there. Orlando, playground or not, was as nice a place as any to spend my time.

One night I took Sheelagh to a party one of my old Front Desk friends was having, and Will came and picked us up from my apartment with Ray and Neil already in the car. The five of us had more fun on the way to the party than we did the entire time we were at it. As I sat amongst my friends, laughing so hard I was practically crying, I thought about how I didn't want to go home; how I'd be happy to stay like this forever, that if these moments were the heights of my Orlando life then that would suit me just fine, I could live with that.

I could live like that.

Nearly eighteen months previously, I had lugged my enormous purple suitcase into the new terminal at Cork International Airport and hoisted it onto the scales, only to be told that it was over the maximum limit for any one piece of luggage. I had to lose two industrial bottles of hair conditioner just so it could be loaded onto my plane, leaving me with thirty-two kilograms worth of possessions and unmanageable hair.

Surveying my bedroom in our Orlando apartment, I doubted very much I'd be able to fit everything back into that one suitcase. Now that I would be travelling to Guatemala instead of coming home, I had no choice but to ship back to Ireland whichever possessions I wanted to keep. Every dollar I spent on shipping was a dollar less I had available to spend in Central America, and could mean the difference between a private room in a nice hostel and a dorm bed riddled with bed bugs. I had to be utterly ruthless in deciding what to keep.

The big items – my bed, for example – had to be sold, so I threw a couple of ads up on Facebook. All the things I had purchased during the Great Bedroom Decoration of February '07 could be left behind - I felt I'd got my money's worth out of my Urban Outfitters bed linen, Target butterfly shower curtain and twenty-dollar flat pack bookcase. My closet was a different story because I'd recently developed an American Eagle Outfitters problem, and now on every hanger there was a brightly-coloured T-shirt or tank from the store's spring collection. Even with my monstrous eighty-litre backpack, I couldn't bring all of them travelling with me, and I doubted I'd have much use for summer clothes back in Ireland, even though it would be summertime when I got home. Then there was my book collection, my photo frames, my souvenirs, my scrap-booking supplies... Boy, this packing thing was hard.

Selling the Mirage proved far easier than buying it had been. On one unseasonably cold day during my last week, Sheelagh and I took it to a CarMax outlet near the airport. I had paid $2,000 for it a year ago, and now I was hoping to get at least a thousand of that back, but the car's condition had deteriorated. A couple of months ago, brake fluid had leaked all over the left rear wheel well; the 'Check Engine' light had been on for the last eight weeks; and the CD player refused to function in warm weather, only coming to life in the dead of night.

But my biggest worry was the lacklustre air conditioning, because you just couldn't sell a car in Central Florida that didn't have ice cold A/C.

Sheelagh and I sat in an office and waited for the magic amount CarMax would buy my car for to appear on a screen. Having both recently read *The Secret*, we desperately tried to visualise a healthy number. After fifteen minutes or so, the results were in: CarMax was going to give me $1,200. This was far more than I had expected, and meant I had only paid $800 to have a car for the last year. Listed beneath the amount were the reasons for this sum and one of them was 'cold A/C.' What CarMax didn't realise was that my air conditioning system took its cue from the temperature outside, and was only blowing cold because it was an unusually cold day.

With a day to go before I left Florida, I managed to reduce my possessions to the backpack I was bringing to Central America and three large boxes I was having shipped home. After the courier company came to pick up the cartons, there was nothing left in my bedroom but a backpack, an air mattress, and a girl getting ready to start looking for what she needed somewhere else.

I spent my last night in Florida as I had spent my first - on the Boardwalk.

Since Jellyrolls had become our favourite haunt, Andrea and I deemed it the most suitable place to meet for a few goodbye drinks. I almost managed to make it through the entire night with my feigned indifference intact, breaking only momentarily when the pianists played my favourite Jellyrolls song, one that would forever remind me of Orlando, Elton John's 'Tiny Dancer'; and afterwards wished 'Catherine good luck on her last night in the United States'. Outside on the promenade, piped musak played and fairy lights twinkled; in the distance, fireworks exploded across the night sky.

Three months from now, I'd be back in Ireland opening the cartons I'd shipped home from Florida, sorting through Mickey Mouse-shaped frames, photos of smiling faces and all sorts of other evidence that I had found happiness in the happiest place on earth.

And I would wish that I were back there.

The previous December, I'd opted out of a second Floridian Christmas and flown home for it instead.

On the way, Andrea and I had fit in a few days in New York, which is how I found myself taking an airport shuttle from our Times Square Hotel to Newark Airport. Next to me on the bus were an Irish woman and her daughter returning home to Cork after a shopping trip, and we got to chatting.

'Were you just in New York on a holiday?' she asked me.

'Well, no...actually I live in Florida.'

'Florida? What do you do down there?'

'I work in Walt Disney World.'

'Disney World? Really? What made you do that?'

'I don't know really. I guess it was just something I always wanted to do.'

'And had you lived away from home before you went there, or was it your first time?'

'No, I lived in Holland for a year before that.'

'Holland? What did you do there?'

'I worked for a kind of travel company.'

'My god.' The woman was shaking her head. She nudged her napping daughter beside her and said, 'Are you listening to this? That girl there is from Cork, and she works in Disney World in Florida. Disney World!' She turned back to me. 'And here we are, meeting you on your way back to Ireland after being in New York. Well, aren't you very *interesting*!'

I had to smile.

Epilogue

It's been three and a half years since I moved to Orlando, and two since I left.

Sheelagh and I had some great times in Central America, met some wonderful people and saw some truly amazing sights. We also didn't wear make-up or use a blow-dryer the entire time we were there, and coming after eighteen months of humidity, chlorine and bleach, you can imagine what state my hair was in by the time I got back home.

In January 2009, Sheelagh moved to New Zealand for her next adventure.

Last April, Eva and I went back to Orlando for a ten-day visit. We managed to do all our favourite things, including Wishes, all the Disney parks, Jellyrolls, Press 101 and Kennedy Space Centre, and hope to go back later this year and do it all over again.

After stints in Canada and Dubai, Eva went back to Germany and, as I write this, is preparing for a move to Salzburg, Austria. We're also planning our Return to Orlando 2010.

Andrea now lives in Washington D.C. Last July, during the fortieth anniversary celebrations of the *Apollo 11* lunar landing, she generously queued at the Smithsonian's Air and Space Museum to get my favourite Apollo astronaut, *Apollo 12's* Alan Bean, to sign a copy of his new book for me. She also sends me Oreo Cakesters; still being a brilliant roommate, four thousand miles away.

The 'Duck and Tuna' is still there of course, as are many of the wonderful friends I made within its walls during my Floridian adventure. (And they were nice enough to upgrade us when we went back as guests!) What *has* changed, however, is the way they handle J-1s. Nowadays you're put to work straight away as opposed to waiting weeks for your Social. Not only does this help you to make friends sooner, it also means your first paycheck arrives promptly, making it easier to not end up living in a glorified squatter's den with seven people who don't speak English, at least four of whom aren't even supposed to be there. While I've blocked out most of my Housekeeping experience, I have nothing but good memories of Front Desk and would happily go back there if Immigration allowed. As for the Rotunda Lobby, the walkway across the Crescent Lake, the hotel's facade floodlit by night - it all still takes my breath away.

But for now I'm back in gloomy Ireland, wishing I could wake up tomorrow morning to a beautiful blue sky, jump in my little Mirage and drive to Celebration for a baked potato omelette and a read of the *Celebration News* in the Market Street Cafe.

Maybe one day.

Maybe.

If there's one experience that sums up, for me, how fantastic Orlando was, it's the one that occurred in the Rocket Garden of Kennedy Space Centre in August 2007, only a few days after my brother John had returned to Ireland.

The sun had set on a balmy summer's day. I was sitting on a folding chair emblazoned with NASA logos, watching an outdoor screening of the movie *Armageddon*, parts of which were filmed on location in KSC. Behind the assembled crowd they were packing away a stage on which, earlier in the evening, Hollywood actor and *Armageddon* star Bruce Willis had performed a concert with his Blues Band. As an annual pass holder I hadn't even had to pay to attend this event, I'd just had to show up.

I'd come to Florida for fun, pixie dust, sun and the States and I'd (eventually!) got all of them. But what I couldn't have known about was all the other things I'd get to do while I was there, such as seeing Bruce Willis sing amidst a floodlit garden of NASA rockets.

It was those things – watching Wishes, sitting by Celebration lake, singing along to 'Tiny Dancer' in Jellyrolls, seeing a Space Shuttle launch – that made it an experience I'll always treasure and never, ever forget.

Well, that and all the Starbucks.

THE END

Further Reading

Walt Disney World Resort:
Married to the Mouse: Walt Disney World and Orlando,
Richard E. Foglesong, Yale University Press, 2001.
Disney War: The Battle for the Magic Kingdom, James B.
Stewart, Simon and Schuster, 2006.

Celebration, FL:
The Celebration Chronicles, Andrew Ross, Ballantine,
1999.
Celebration U.S.A., Douglas Franz and Catherine Collins,
Henry Holt & Co., 1999.

NASA and the Apollo Program:
A Man on the Moon, Andrew Chaikin, Penguin Books,
1998.
Apollo, Charles Murray and Catherine Cox, South
Mountain Books, 2004.
Moondust: In Search of the Men Who Fell to Earth,
Andrew Smith, Bloomsbury, 2005.

Atheism:
The God Delusion, Prof. Richard Dawkins, Houghton
Mifflin, 2006.
The End of Faith, Sam Harris, W.W. Norton & Co., 2004.

Central Florida in Fiction:
All Families are Psychotic, Douglas Coupland, Harper
Perennial, 2001.
The Time It Takes To Fall, Margaret Lazarus Dean,
Simon & Schuster, 2007.

Working Abroad:
Work Your Way Around the World, Susan Griffith,
Crimson Publishing, 2009.

THE SANE PERSON'S GUIDE TO WALT DISNEY WORLD

Walt Disney World is a place of happiness, magic and wonder, but a family visit there can also induce a nervous breakdown and sow the seeds of divorce. Drawing on her experience as a WDW Front Desk Agent and her own visits to the theme parks, Catherine dispenses Disney World advice in easy-to-swallow, Mickey-shaped chewable tablets, the theme being 'Relax – and that's an order!' Sprinkled with sarcasm and fun but useless facts (did you know, for example, that Magic Kingdom's trash is emptied every fifteen minutes?), Catherine's Disney guide provides just the right amount of information for a magical Mouse visit, the kind of family vacation your children will *not* be recalling for a mental health professional some day in the far off future.

The Sane Person's Guide includes everything you need to know about Walt Disney World, but not as much as a particle of pixie dust more.

- ✓ **Mouse Manuals**: Do you need one and if so, which one?
- ✓ **Disney World 101**: Everything you need to know before you go
- ✓ **Into the Parks**: A quick run down of each of Disney World's four theme parks
- ✓ **The Other Stuff**: There's more to Disney than theme parks and mice, don't ya know
- ✓ **Frequently Asked Questions**: What time IS the 3 o'clock parade?

Visit **www.mousetrappedbook.com**
to view Catherine's photo albums and videos
and to download your FREE e-book edition of
The Sane Person's Guide to Walt Disney World.

Want Your Own Yummy Adventure?

Contact Yummy Jobs of London for your chance to put your skills to use in the hospitality, tourism or leisure industry and embark on the adventure of a lifetime in the United States, Canada, Australia or India.

They recruit for:

- Disney's International Programs
- American Hotel Resort Programs
- Summer Lovin' USA Program
- Yummy Canada
- Yummy Australia
- Yummy Volunteer in India
- Study Abroad

They recruit from the United Kingdom, Ireland, The Netherlands, Switzerland, Canada and beyond!

Go to **www.yummyjobs.com**
or contact **enquiries@yummyjobs.com**

Acknowledgements

Thanks Mum and Dad for everything, John for all the timely cups of tea and Claire for her careful monitoring of our Sky Plus.

Sheelagh Kelly - For being the best friend a gal can have and for not making fun of my pseudo-American accent when you came to stay. V.O. x

Eva Heppel, for saving me from my Orlando pity party and those infamous driving lessons, and Andrea Summers for being such a brilliant roommate and Apollo astronaut hunter. Thank you both for everything, then and now, and I'll see you in Jellyrolls for a round of 32oz cocktails... x

Iain Harris - Oh, the hair/pointy shoes/vests/casual blazer jokes I could immortalise in print here! But I'll resist. Instead I'll just say: Treacle. (Happy now?)

Everyone at the, ahem, Duck and Tuna (!), especially Candi Young (Manager/Space Shuttle Fairy Godmother extraordinaire), Steve Carrion, (Pretend Brother/Long Island Ice Tea drinking buddy/Nickname Generator extraordinaire), Kevin Karson, David Volpe and Spencer Sigall (collectively lunchmates/gossip gang extraordinaire), John Ortiz (Rooms Control/FD Dream Team member extraordinaire), Katarzyna Horta (coffee-at-The-Loop-buddy extraordinaire), Kim Marchetti and Todd Spence (Training Team/Welcome Committee extraordinaires) and everyone else in the Front Desk and Housekeeping Departments. Were I to name everyone the list would be too long but you know who you are. Thank you each for everything and I hope to see you all soon. xxx

Thanks also to Andrew and Rebecca Brown, Emma Birmingham, Laura Dougal, Hannah Ferguson, Sarah Franklin, Claire Gribben, Ben Johncock, Peggy Murray, Vanessa O'Loughlin, Séan Ó Floinn, Jane Travers, David Thuillier, Aisling White and the team at Yummy Jobs.

Thanks to John Dixon, for giving me not only the idea to write this book but its name as well.

I feel I should really thank John Mayer for making great music to write to (even if he did make me cry on a Disney bus), Starbucks at the Premium Outlets on Vineland Avenue for making venti lattes just the way I like 'em and whoever invented Oreo Cakesters (you are a genius).

(Mum: look away now.) To the two people whose rental cars I accidentally, ah, *bumped* into with my Mirage: thank you for not calling the cops. (Did I not mention I was involved in not one but two fender-benders? Oops. My mistake.) Had you done so, this book might have been called *Deported* instead. (FYI: Crying works every time.)

Thanks to all my Twitter and Facebook friends who have helped with this book and, last but not least, thank YOU for reading this, you little star!

8285893R0